COLLECTOR'S GUIDE TO

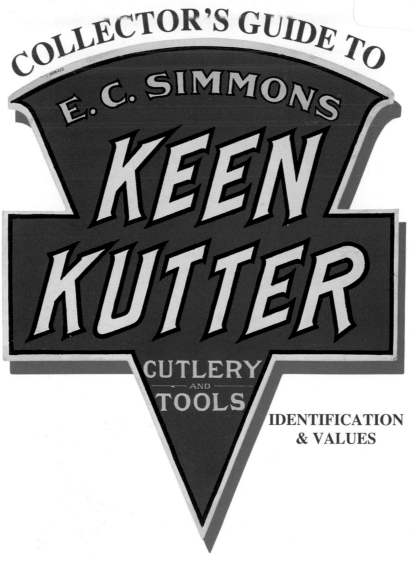

E. C. SIMMONS

KEEN KUTTER

CUTLERY AND TOOLS

IDENTIFICATION & VALUES

Jerry and Elaine Heuring

COLLECTOR BOOKS

A Division of Schroeder Publishing Co., Inc.

The current values in this book should be used only as a guide. They are not intended to set prices, which vary from one section of the country to another. Auction prices as well as dealer prices vary greatly and are affected by condition as well as demand. Neither the authors nor the publisher assumes responsibility for any losses that might be incurred as a result of consulting this guide.

Cover design: Michelle Dowling
Book design: Karen Geary

Searching For A Publisher?

We are always looking for knowledgeable people considered to be experts within their fields. If you feel that there is a real need for a book on your collectible subject and have a large comprehensive collection, contact Collector Books.

COLLECTOR BOOKS
P.O. Box 3009
Paducah, KY 42002-3009

Copyright © 2000 by Jerry and Elaine Heuring

CONTENTS

E.C. SIMMONS
KEEN KUTTER
CUTLERY AND TOOLS

DEDICATION

I would like to dedicate this book to my wife Elaine. If it weren't for her, there would be no Keen Kutter book. For three years she has pushed me to get the book done. There have been starts and stops over the last three years. Just trying to get the pictures developed was a big challenge because they had to be just perfect. There have been several arguments, but she never gave up on me. She was sick for several years, but never complained. She just tries to keep me going because Keen Kutter has always been "our" collection. She has always said if the Keen Kutter collection goes, she goes with it. So it looks like we will always have our collection. She never quit or gave up like I wanted to several times. She did all the descriptions, research, and organized all the pictures. All I did was take the pictures and set the values. She gets all the credit from me for getting this book done. If I would go on and on about how much Elaine does, there would be an endless list. She is the best and there is not another one like her who would put up with me. She is my whole life along with Wendy, our daughter, and Craig, our son-in-law.

ABOUT THE AUTHORS

Jerry and Elaine, high school sweethearts from the small town of Kelso in southeast Missouri, were married in 1970. Jerry accepted an industrial arts teaching position in Fayette, Missouri, in 1972. For leisure on weekends they attended auctions and soon caught the contagious antique fever.

With the desire to start a family and build a new home, Jerry left his teaching position for the carpentry industry. Elaine was employed in clerical positions at various lumberyards, so the tool industry has always been a part of their lives.

In 1974, their daughter Wendy was born. Wendy grew up in an environment influenced by antiques. She developed an eye for antiques early in her life, and one of the most memorable adventures is when Wendy found their Keen Kutter sewing machine. Wendy and her husband Craig are still very interested in antiques.

In 1976, Jerry and Elaine owned a large variety of tools ranging from Keen Kutter, Winchester, and Stanley. At that time, Keen Kutter tools were still going for reasonable prices; that, along with the beautiful logo, encouraged them to start a Keen Kutter collection. They continued to purchase other brands for resale purposes and still do today.

This is their third price guide on Keen Kutter with several upgrades of the second edition. As in any collection, the condition of any item is critical in determining its value. If the name or logo is battered or unreadable, the value will be considerably less than if it were good to mint condition. For example, a regular claw hammer with the logo in good condition would be a $35.00 hammer; but, if that logo was scratched or unreadable, it could be worth $5.00. The items in their collection are in very good to mint condition.

Jerry and Elaine value their collection and enjoy the opportunity to share it with you. Because of their collection they have made many valuable acquaintances and look forward to making many more.

There is life other than Keen Kutter for them also. Among the hobbies Jerry and Elaine share in addition to quality time with their family are involvement in church functions, deer hunting, camping, reading, going to antique markets, and working on the computer.

In the back of this value guide you will find information on the Mid-West Tool Collectors Association, Inc. (M-WTCA) and The Hardware Companies Kollectibles Klub (THCKK).

Jerry and Elaine's wish for you — "HAPPY HUNTING."

ACKNOWLEDGMENTS

We are honored once again to share our Keen Kutter collection with you. This would not be possible without the confidence Collector Books has expressed in us throughout the past 16 years. A special thanks is extended to Lisa Stroup of Collector Books editorial staff for her assistance, patience, and encouragement through the trying times of putting all the pieces together

The most trying experience was finding someone who cared as much as we did in achieving a clear detailed photo finish. A very special thank you to that person, Jim Keeney from the Camera Shop in Paducah, Kentucky, for his expertise in developing the majority of our photos. We also want to thank his assistant, Judy Ayers, for her help. A special thank you to Doug Adams of Cape Girardeau, Missouri, for his advice on lighting and camera details.

A special thanks is extended to you, our customers, for purchasing our value guides. We also want to thank each and every one of you who has allowed us the opportunity to purchase from you. Perhaps as you look through this book you might find an item that you once owned. The only time an item leaves our collection is when it is a duplicate item or when we are upgrading. We thank anyone who has given us that opportunity to add to our collection and look forward to dealing with many of you again.

We want to thank the members of M-WTCA and THCKK for showing their support by keeping the prices alive at various tool meets. Also a special thanks to Simmons & Company Auctioneers, Inc. of Richmond, Missouri, and other auction companies for providing opportunities for collectors to upgrade their collections. Information regarding membership in these two organizations can be found at the back of this value guide.

A special thank you for their patience and love is extended to our daughter Wendy and son-in-law Craig as well as to other immediate family members who probably feel we have been putting Keen Kutter ahead of them for the past few years while compiling this value guide.

And finally thank you, Wendy, for the wonderful memories you just keep on giving us. When we arrived home from a weekend buying trip several years ago, we found a batch of cookies shaped like the Keen Kutter logo. Wendy had gone to the local hardware store and asked what she could make a cookie cutter out of. That cookie cutter has been used many times and always brings a smile to anyone who likes either Keen Kutter or cookies.

HISTORY

THE FOUNDERS

Edward Campbell Simmons, 1839 – 1921

E. C. Simmons, known as "No. 8" because the letter "S" in his signature looked like the figure "8", established Simmons Hardware Company which was one of the most extensive corporations of its kind in the West. He was born in Frederick County, Maryland, on September 21, 1839. In 1846, his father, a merchant, moved the family to St. Louis, Missouri. E. C. entered the wholesale hardware establishment of Child, Pratt & Company in 1856 at the age of 17 at a salary of $12.50 per month. Three years later, he became a clerk for Wilson, Leavering & Waters at a salary of $50.00 per month and by 1862 became a junior partner. At the end of six months, Mr. Leavering died and the name of the firm was changed to Waters, Simmons & Company.

In 1866, Simmons and Carrie Welsh were married. Waters, Simmons & Company continued through nine years of great prosperity. In 1870, Simmons chose Keen Kutter as the brand name for the company's line of high grade tools and cutlery. Mr. Waters retired January 1, 1872, and Simmons in association with J. W. Morton established the firm of E. C. Simmons & Company. Two years later, a corporation was formed under the name of the Simmons Hardware Company, which purchased the interests of E. C. Simmons & Company. Simmons believed in close personal contact with both customers and employees showing interest in their prosperity and welfare. From this commitment the phrase, *"A jobber's first duty is to help his customers to prosper"* was the slogan in the first jobber's catalog of 1881 and became known as E. C. Simmons' Golden Rule. Simmons retired from active management in 1897 at age 58, relinquishing the company to his three sons: George W. Simmons, Wallace D. Simmons, and Edward H. Simmons.

August Frederick Shapleigh, 1810 – 1902

Augustus Frederick Shapleigh was born January 9, 1810, in Portsmouth, New Hampshire. At the age of 14, he worked for one year at a hardware store in Portsmouth from daylight to dark for $50.00. For a three-year period, A. F. Shapleigh left the hardware store to lead a sailor's life. Soon after returning, he accepted an important clerkship job with Rogers Brothers & Company, a wholesale hardware dealer in Philadelphia. He worked with them for many years and obtained a junior partnership. Shapleigh was sent to St. Louis, Missouri, in 1843 to open a branch establishment of which he served as superintendent. The firm was called Rogers, Shapleigh & Company. Upon Mr. Roger's death, Shapleigh formed a connection with Thomas D. Day under the firm name of Shapleigh, Day & Company in 1847, which existed for 16 years. When Mr. Day retired in 1863, the company became A. F. Shapleigh & Company. In 1864, the company adopted Diamond Edge as the brand name for a line of superior tools and cutlery. Shapleigh retired in 1901 and died a year later.

THE COMPANY

The Winchester-Simmons merger was announced on June 26, 1922, at the second annual convention of the National Association of Winchester Clubs in New Haven. The new organization was known as the Winchester Simmons Company. They had about 2,000 agents at the time of the merger which grow to over 6,000 by 1927. The Winchester Repeating Arms Co. had four branch houses located in Kansas City, Missouri; Atlanta, Georgia; Chicago, Illinois; and San Francisco, California. The Simmons Hardware Company had seven branch houses located in St. Louis, Missouri; Toledo, Ohio; Minneapolis, Minnesota; Philadelphia, Pennsylvania; Boston, Massachusetts; Sioux City, Iowa; and Wichita, Kansas. Many of the Winchester agents were not loyal to their company and spent money unwisely on advertising and entertainment. On March 9, 1929, announcement was made of the termination of the Winchester Agency Plan. The Simmons Hardware Company reverted to its original status and the name Winchester no longer appeared in conjunction with the name Simmons.

As a result of negotiations in the spring of 1940, Shapleigh Hardware Company purchased for cash all assets of Simmons Hardware Company, effective July 1, 1940. Proceeds of the sale were distributed to stockholders of the Simmons Hardware Company whose charter was surrendered in due time. Shapleigh Hardware Company occupied all the buildings used by Simmons Hardware Company at Ninth & Spruce Streets in St. Louis as well as additional facilities on Poplar, Seventh to Eighth Streets. A majority of the Simmons Hardware Company personnel became associated with Shapleigh Hardware Company. All Simmons Hardware Company trademarked lines were continued and the business, thus greatly enlarged, operated smoothly and successfully under Shapleigh's management until its closing in the early 1960s.

In 1962, Russell Cook, the former stores program manager of the Shapleigh Hardware Company, was asked by Carl Dixson, president of the Brown-Rogers-Dixson Hardware Sales Company, Winston-Salem, North Carolina, to take over the Val-Test Distributors Buying Group. Cook agreed, and while looking for financial backing, he ran into

BRIEF HISTORY

1847
Shapleigh, Day & Company established.

1863
A. F. Shapleigh & Company established.

1870
Keen Kutter name chosen by E. C. Simmons.

1872
E. C. Simmons & Company established.

1874
Simmons Hardware Company established.

1922
Winchester-Simmons Company established.

1929
Simmons Hardware Company reverted to original status.

1940
Shapleigh Hardware Company established.

1962
Val-Test Distributors Buying Group still existing.

Mark Long, eventual liquidator of the Shapleigh Co. The two men agreed that Long would put up $5,000 for working capital, and Val-Test would market the Keen Kutter name on hardware products through the Val-Test Group. Long leased the use of Keen Kutter to Val-Test in 1962. Other trademarks such as Diamond Edge were part of the package. After Long's death, the Keen Kutter trademark was tied up in a trust fund for 25 years until it was finally purchased by Val-Test who still owns it today.

CATALOGS

Shapleigh's first catalog was issued in 1853, a small paperback with no illustrations. By 1880, both Simmons Hardware Company and A. F. Shapleigh & Company published large, well-bound general line catalogs. These catalogs, with the sole exception of one issued by Markley, Alling & Company of Chicago, were the first of their type to make an appearance in the hardware trade of the United States. At frequent intervals up until 1912, revised catalogs were distributed. Net prices were listed from time to time. The Simmons Hardware Company 1912 catalog was the first annual catalog containing prices on each item. Market changes made it necessary and it was found to be more practical to print price revised catalogs rather than reprint the entire catalog. Prosperous years followed for both Simmons Hardware Company and A. F. Shapleigh & Company. Their trade areas steadily expanded and eventually the combined sales of the two companies attained so large a volume as to firmly establish St. Louis as the largest distributor of hardware in the nation.

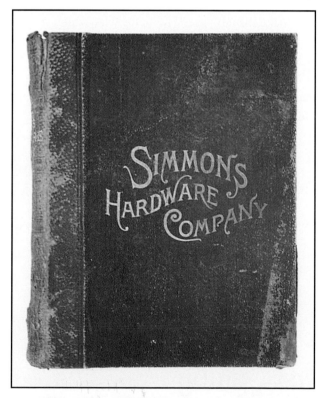

Jan. 20, 1899 catalog, leather bound. Containing 1,768 pages with index, it is 4" thick, weighs 16 lbs., has 8,350 illustrations; 12,000 copies were printed, using 6 car loads of paper and 13½ tons tar boards, 11,000 sq. ft. leather, and 24,000 sq. yds. cloth, taking 14 months for binding, delivered in 650 cases, requiring 110 wagon loads.

TRADEMARK & MOTTO

TRADEMARK

Every Keen Kutter tool was tested and inspected before being stamped with the trademark. The name and trademark, whether in logo form or words, were the marker's promise of superior quality. This promise was for the consumer's protection and guaranteed perfection or money refunded.

E. C. Simmons originated the house motto, *"The Recollection Of Quality Remains Long After The Price Is Forgotten,"* in 1898 while on vacation in Oconomowoc, Wisconsin. Simmons was especially pleased with a good shave he received at a barber shop there and asked to see the excellent razor. After inspecting it, Mr. Simmons asked what the barber paid for the razor. The barber answered, "I do not remember the price, but I will never forget the quality." Leaving the shop, those words rang in Mr. Simmons ears, and he evolved the house slogan. This slogan is often seen as "TROQRLATPIF."

The Keen Kutter name first appeared on an axe in 1866. In the early days, the Lippincott axe was very popular, being thinner in the blade, thus cutting better in soft woods. The manufacturers would charge any good retail buyer the same prices they would sell to Simmons' wholesale house. Simmons sought some protection from the head of the axe factory, but none was forthcoming. That night, Mr. Simmons went home angry and disturbed. During the night, he woke up thinking axes. He got up, hunted a block of wood, and with his pen knife whittled out a long, slim axe, slimmer than the Lippincott. When finished, he wrote in pencil on the fresh pine wooden axe, "KEEN KUTTER." The next day, he found a manufacturer to make his new axe. The favor with which they were received by the trade encouraged the immediate development of an extensive line of Keen Kutter tools and cutlery. The Keen Kutter name was adopted as a logo by Simmons Hardware Company in 1870.

Prior to the now-famous Keen Kutter logo, there was a shield type logo (*Fig. 1*) which can be found in the 1899 catalog. This logo seemed to appear mainly on axes and adzes, postcards, and invoices. Another used prior to 1900 emblem was the name written out in banner style (*Fig. 2*).

There was also a sawtooth-type emblem, some rectangular ones around 1891 (*Fig. 3*), and some circular shapes around 1900 (*Fig. 4*), which appeared on plane irons and wood chisels.

Planes, both iron and wood bottom varieties, marked by Simmons Hardware Company with the "KK" design from 1905 – 1913 were made by Ohio Tool Co. Starting in 1914, the single "K" was used and those planes were made by Stanley.

The Keen Kutter trademark of 1905 shows a block of wood with a wedge being driven into it with the words "St. Louis, USA". In 1912, the words "Cutlery & Tools" (*Fig. 5*) were used. This is the emblem most familiar; it continued even after Simmons sold to Shapleigh in 1940 and was used until the 1960s.

Fig. 1

Fig. 2

Fig. 3

Fig. 4

Fig. 5

In 1962, Russell Cook, former stores program manager for Shapleigh Hardware, took over the Val-Test Distributors Buying Group. With financial backing from Mark Long, Val-Test marketed hardware using the Keen Kutter name. Long leased the name to Val-Test. Some of the logos had Shapleigh written above Keen Kutter which is on the large "K" (*Fig. 6*). After being tied up for 25 years in a trust fund, Val-Test Distributors purchased the Keen Kutter trademark and still use it today, but it will only have the words Keen Kutter in it. Their main logo is with the large K and wedge (*Fig. 7*).

Often the words Keen Kutter were all that appeared. For example, sometimes on files, garden tools, and augers, Keen Kutter would be written with a large "K" being used for first letter in both words, as in the socket firmer chisel sample. (*Fig. 8*).

It appears Simmons substituted a "K" for the "C" in Cutter to get a more percussive sound. The "KK" format is used on different types of products by Simmons line such as King Koaster (child wagon), Klipper Klub (ice skates), Korn & Koffee Krushers, Karpet King (sweeper), Kool King (ice box), Klear Krystal (lamp chimney), Kar King, Keen Klipper (lawn mower), Klincher (mouse traps and locks), and Keen Kaster (fishing reel).

Fig. 6

Fig. 7

Fig. 8

MOTTO

"We guarantee this tool to be properly made and tempered, and that the steel is free from manufacturing defects. If found otherwise and returned to us we will give a new one for it." — Keen Kutter Guarantee.

The Keen Kutter line was more than just so many tools. It was a complete line carefully planned and built to serve a very definite purpose, to make easier the job of the retailer and user. E. C. Simmons said, "A jobber's first duty is to help his customer to prosper." Throughout the Keen Kutter catalogs and "want books," many phrases describing the product line exist, such as:

KEEN KUTTER — The correct tool for every job.

Tools that work. Tools that are reliable. Tools that are ready when you are. Tools that will do hard work on hard material. Such tools are Keen Kutter quality tools.

Keen Kutter — The hardware brand for every demand.

A cutting edge for a generation. In cutlery your ideal of yesterday is the nation's choice of today. There is no substitute for Keen Kutter.

Every customer since 1894 a satisfied customer.

When in doubt, don't guess, just buy a Keen Kutter.

Keen Kutter tools, the best that brains, money, and skill can produce.

They are the finest tools for the finest work. The most accurate tools for the most accurate workman. Keen Kutter quality tools are all the very highest quality, finest tools that can be made.

The better the tool, the better the work. There is one sure way to get the best tool for any purpose, ask for Keen Kutter quality tools.

Keen Kutter tools are made for hard work. Hard work doesn't hurt good tools, and tools to be good must do hard work.

Who were KEEN KUTTER tools made for? For the farmers, lawyers, doctors, and merchants engrossed in the cares of their profession or business, yet frequently love to play at making things and to create with their hands. For the skilled mechanic, who because of his expert knowledge, knows what is good when he sees it. For the boy who loves tools, good tools, pretty tools.

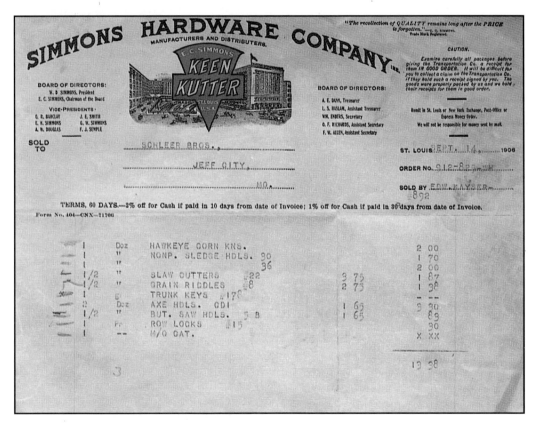

Simmons Hardware Company receipt dated Sept. 14, 1906.

ADVERTISING

Neon sign, 30" long x 5½", $1,750.00 – 2,000.00.

Electric display sign, E. C. Simmons Keen Kutter Store, metal with masonite back and wooden letters, contains four light bulbs. 31½" long x 5½" tall x 4½" wide, $700.00 – 900.00.

1' double-sided porcelain emblem-shaped sign which went on the side of buildings or stores, has some chips; as is, $900.00 – 1,200.00; mint, $1,750.00 – 2,000.00.

Porcelain double-sided flanged "We Sell" sign, 27½" x 18", same wording on both sides, has chips; as is, $500.00 – 750.00; excellent condition, $1,500.00 – 2,000.00.

E. C. Simmons Paints advertising sign, hanging porcelain double-sided round, 13½" diameter, both sides are identical. As is, $500.00 – 750.00; excellent condition, $1,500.00 – 1,700.00.

Round electric store window clock, #KKEC, red enameled 18¾" with a 15" white dial. This clock was given free to any dealer buying $300.00 or more in a single order of Keen Kutter. The dealer could purchase the clock for $35.00 with a minimum order. As is, $1,100.00 – 1,300.00. With original stand, $2,000.00.

Hardware advertising sign used on buildings, fences, etc., 9¾" x 27¾". Has the store name and location, very colorful, $125.00 – 175.00.

Store identification sign, plastic, 2' x 4', double sided with a fluorescent bulb in between (only one side shown). As is, $100.00 – 150.00; complete, $500.00 – 600.00.

Electric clock, 15"x15" square, #K530. This clock was placed in store windows to attract the attention of passersby who daily checked the time, $700.00 – 875.00.

Shapleigh's electric clock, 10" round plastic. $275.00 – 350.00.

Round thermometer, temperature goes from -30° to 120°, *authentic*, $250.00 – 325.00. (See reproduction are page 183.)

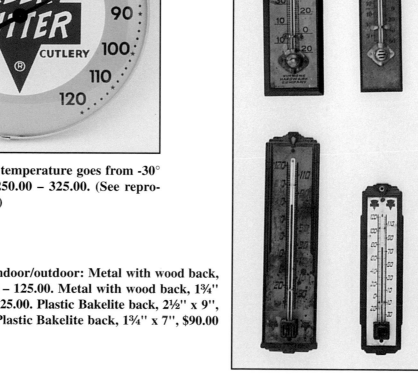

Thermometers, indoor/outdoor: Metal with wood back, 2½" x 9", $90.00 – 125.00. Metal with wood back, 1¾" x 7½", $90.00 – 125.00. Plastic Bakelite back, 2½" x 9", $90.00 – 125.00. Plastic Bakelite back, 1¾" x 7", $90.00 – 125.00.

Hand fan, fold-out with large logo on one side, side not shown contains a floral design, $250.00 – 350.00.

Hand fan, 1904 World's Fair, St. Louis, Missouri Exhibit. Photo shows both sides, one being the old shield emblem; the other, the exhibit. Wooden handle resembles axe handle, $175.00 – 275.00.

Hand fan, St. Louis 1904 World's Fair, showing Keen Kutter Headquarters on one side and a hatchet with the old shield emblem on the other, $175.00 – 275.00.

Back and front of two different hand fans. One with logo is advertisement for Jackson, Missouri, $75.00 – 125.00; house scene is advertisement for Halstead, Kansas, $75.00 – 125.00.

Left:
Sewing kit containing two spools of thread, needles, thimble. Has hardware store name on front, $125.00 – 175.00.

Right:
Matchbooks, one side has emblem and other side store advertisement, $15.00 – 20.00 each.

Left: Pen and pencil set with case, $200.00 – 275.00. Right: Pen and pencil sets. $125.00 – 175.00 per set.

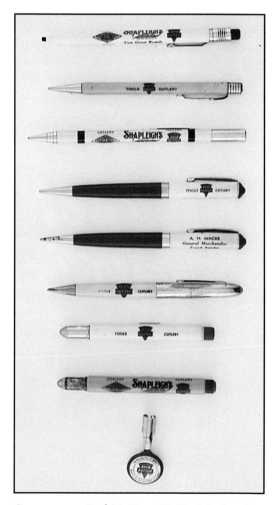

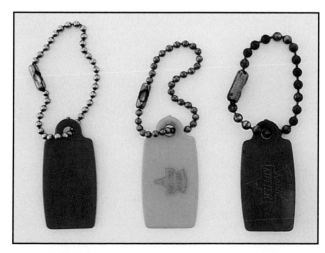

Key chains, small plastic with hardware store name on back, $40.00 – 60.00 each.

Grease pencil, $35.00 – 50.00. Mechanical pencil, $30.00 – 50.00 each. Bullet pencil, $35.00 – 45.00 each. Pencil clip, $7.50 – 10.00.

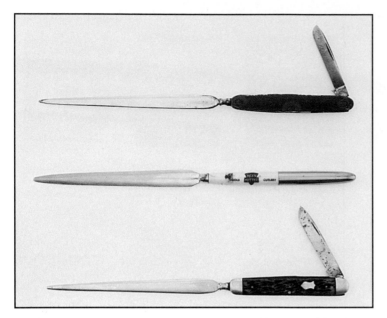

Top: Letter opener with leather handle, logo on knife blade, $125.00 – 200.00. Middle: Letter opener with pen on end, store advertisement on handle, $125.00 – 200.00. Bottom: Letter opener with knife, logo on blade, $125.00 – 200.00.

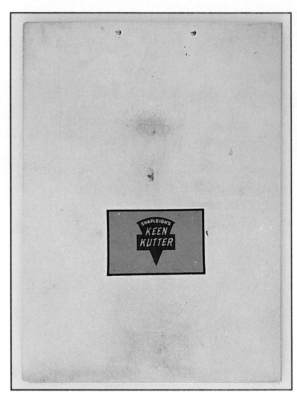

Notebook holder with metal folding clip, 12½" x 9", $75.00 – 100.00.

"Headquarters for Keen Kutter" paper advertising sign (came in set of two). Display size: 21¾" x 15½". One sheet advertises hand tools; the other pocket knives. Each has a white back side. (Another set advertises power mowers and power tools.) $25.00 – 50.00 each set.

Sheet of advertisement art layout, $50.00 – 75.00; Newspaper ad stamps, $35.00 – 55.00 each.

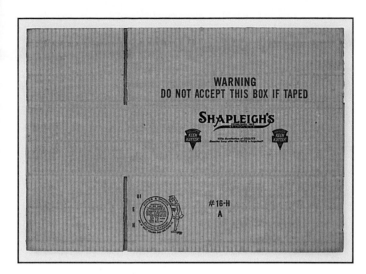

Cardboard box, unused, 13" x 4½", $20.00 – 30.00.

Paper shopping bag with handles, $100.00 – 125.00.

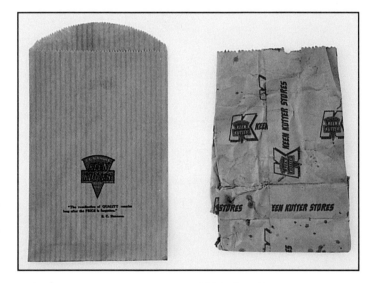

Left: Paper bag, unused, 5" x 8¾", $50.00 – 75.00. Right: Paper bag, used, 4¾" x 7½", $40.00 – 60.00.

Pieces of wrapping paper used in hardware stores. These were all from Missouri. $10.00 – 20.00 each.

Yard sticks, give-aways with hardware store advertisement on them, $25.00 – 35.00 each.

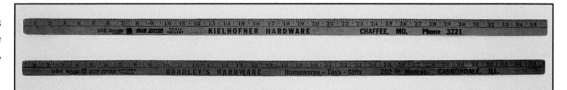
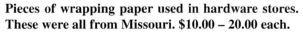

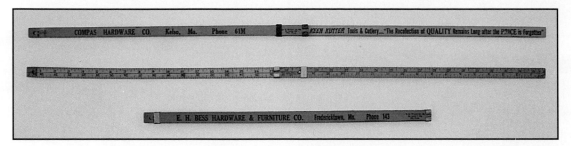

3' sliding rules, store give-aways, can be used as a yard stick or to take an inside measurement (the numbers on half of one side jump from 18" to 36" for inside measurement). Hardware company name and location on other side, $30.00 – 45.00 each.

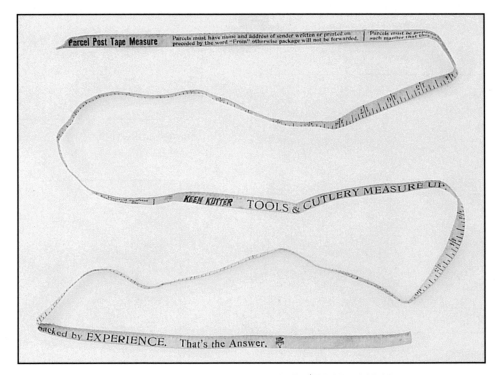

6' parcel post tape measurer, cloth, $75.00 – 125.00.

AXES & HATCHETS

Broad axe, Bob Taylor Canada pattern, E. C. Simmons with large logo with Bob Taylor under logo, 12" cutting edge, $125.00 – 200.00.

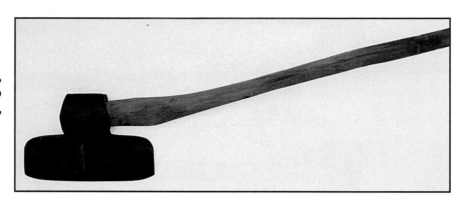

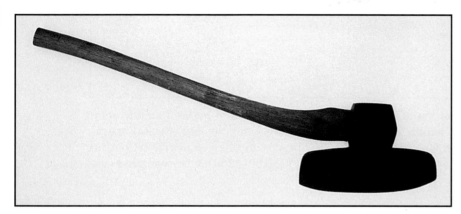

Broad axe, E. C. Simmons with large logo, 13" cutting edge, $125.00 – 200.00.

Broad axe, Keen Kutter written out, 12" cutting edge, $100.00 – 150.00.

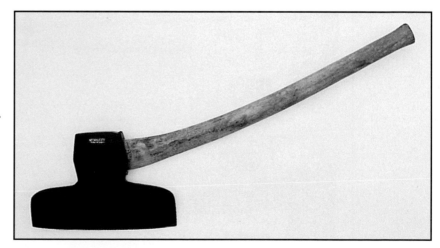

Fireman's axe, large logo, 12¼" overall length, 8¼" length of head, 4" length of point, 5¼" at widest point. $375.00 – 475.00.

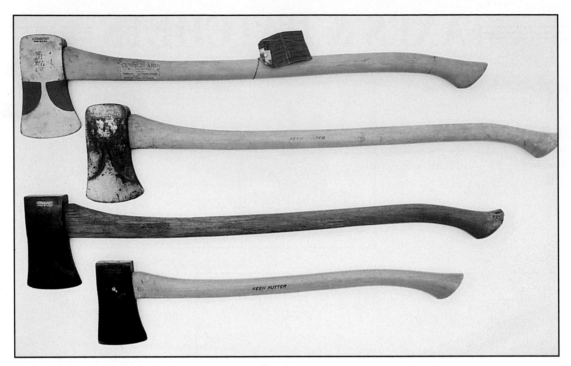

Axes, all Michigan pattern. From top to bottom: Perfect bevel with Cumberland handle, mint condition with original marked handle and paper tag, $100.00 – 150.00; Still can see marks from where paper label was, $100.00 – 150.00; 7¼" x 4½" head with "Keen Kutter" written out on handle, $75.00 – 125.00; Boy's hand axe, mint condition, $150.00 – 200.00. Normal used condition range from $15.00 – 30.00.

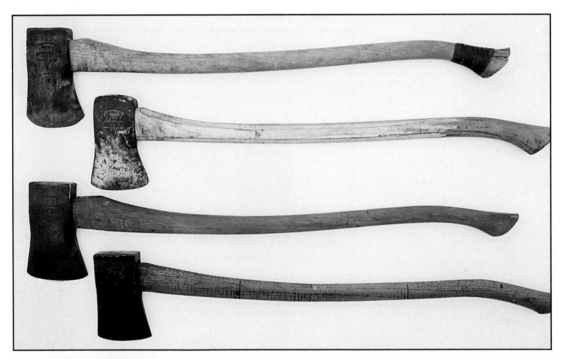

E. C. Simmons axes. From top to bottom: No. 5 Special composite pattern, plain, $50.00 – 75.00; #KMA1 Michigan pattern, octagonal handle, round head, original red paint, $150.00 – 175.00; Dayton pattern, wide head, plain, $50.00 – 75.00; New Yankee pattern, $50.00 – 75.00. Normal used condition, $20.00 – 40.00.

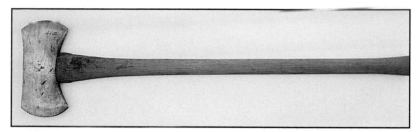

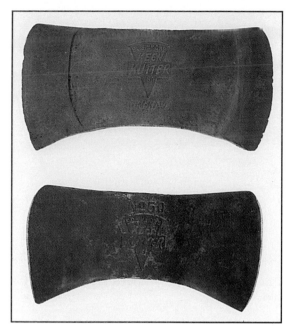

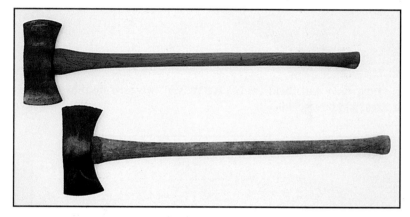

Double bit axe with two small logos, one on each side, unusual mark, $75.00 – 100.00.

Axe head, double bit, Kon-Kave written out under large logo, $40.00 – 60.00. Axe head, double bit, No. 50 stamped above large logo, $40.00 – 60.00.

Double bit axes, sizes 9½" x 4½". Top: Special composite pattern with Keen Kutter written out, $25.00 – 40.00. Bottom: Keen Kutter written out, $25.00 – 40.00.

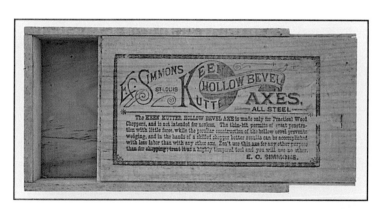

Axe box, sliding top, contained a 4½ lb. hollow bevel axe head. Box size: 9¼" x 5¾" x 2". $125.00 – 175.00.

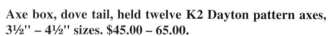

Axe box, dove tail, held twelve K2 Dayton pattern axes, 3½" – 4½" sizes. $45.00 – 65.00.

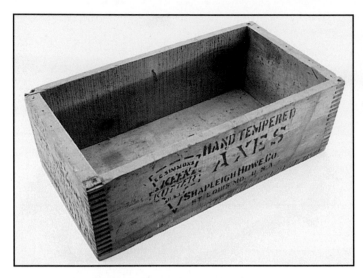

Axe box, dove tail, held twelve KBW 3½'' western double bit axes, $45.00 – 65.00.

Axe box, held 3½'' to 4½'' western style double bit axes, $35.00 – 55.00.

Axe box, held twelve E. C. Simmons KM352 Black Michigan pattern double bit axes, $35.00 – 55.00.

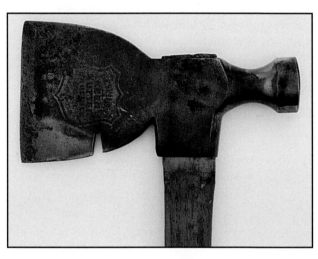

Shingling hatchet, 3¼'' cut with "Shield" emblem found in 1899 catalog, $175.00 – 225.00.

Half hatchet with the original sticker, mint condition. Bottom photo shows the logo marking when sticker is removed, $200.00 – 275.00.

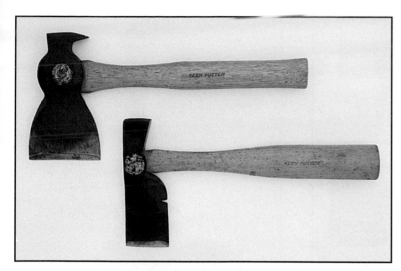

Top: Claw hatchet with label, mint, $200.00 – 275.00. Bottom: Lathing hatchet with label marked "Genuine Underhill," has checkered face and nail slot, mint, $200.00 – 275.00. If sticker were removed the logo would show. Pricing is based on mint with the original paper sticker as shown.

Hatchets with Boy Scout emblem as well as Keen Kutter logo on each of them. The Boy Scout emblem is usually very faint and hard to see. $75.00 – 100.00 each.

Shapleigh sport axe, octagonal handle still has Keen Kutter written on it. Axe has the duck flying off scene with "For Sportsman" written under it. In excellent condition, $300.00 – 375.00.

Left to right: Chromed scout axe, $45.00 – 65.00; Scout axe with notch in it, $30.00 – 40.00; Hunter's axe, $30.00 – 40.00; Small hatchet cut, 2½" x 4¼", $100.00 – 150.00.

Scout axe with just "Keen Kutter" written, $35.00 – 45.00. Child-size hatchet with "Keen Kutter" written on one side and "E. C. Simmons, St. Louis, MO" on the other side. Hatchet 2¼" x 4" long head. $75.00 – 100.00.

Broad or bench head hatchets. Top: 4½" Shapleigh single bevel (flat on one side), $65.00 – 75.00. Bottom: E. C. Simmons double bevel (beveled on both sides), $75.00 – 85.00.

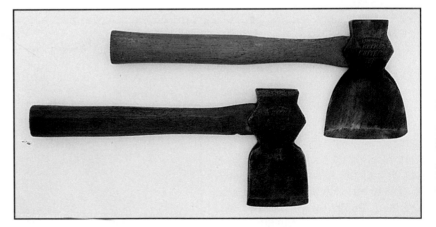

Broad or bench hatchet, single bevel. Top: 4", $65.00 – 75.00. Bottom: 3", $75.00 – 100.00.

E. C. Simmons broad head, single bevel hatchet. Top to bottom: 6", $75.00 – 100.00; 5½", $75.00 – 85.00; 4½", $65.00 – 75.00.

Top: Tommy axe, $70.00 – 85.00. Bottom: Tomahawk belt axe, $70.00 – 85.00.

Top: E. C. Simmons flooring hatchet with nail slot, $45.00 – 55.00. Bottom: E. C. Simmons machinist pattern hatchet, $45.00 – 55.00.

Plain poll claw hatchets, one is E. C. Simmons; the other is Shapleigh. $35.00 – 45.00 each.

Top: Barreling hatchet with special nail slot in blade, has checkered face, $75.00 – 85.00. Bottom: Produce hatchet with special top nail slot, square checkered face, $75.00 – 85.00.

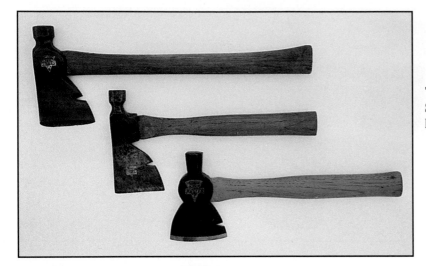

Top: Rig builders hatchet, $45.00 – 55.00. Middle: Shingling hatchet, $35.00 – 45.00. Bottom: Az-eye half hatchet with octagon neck, $35.00 – 45.00.

Top: Chromed lathing hatchet with gauge, has original precut notches and logo on both sides, $75.00 – 100.00. Bottom: Chromed lathing hatchet with logo on both sides, $45.00 – 55.00.

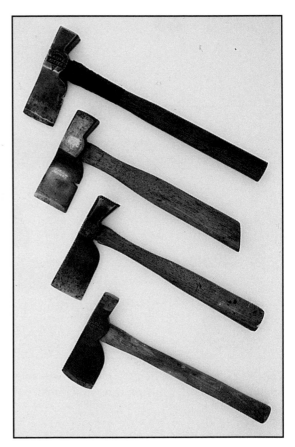

Lathing hatchets. Top to bottom: Lathing hatchet, $30.00 – 40.00; lathing checkered face, genuine Underhill, $30.00 – 40.00; lathing thin blade, California pattern checkered face, $30.00 – 40.00; lathing hatchet, $30.00 – 40.00.

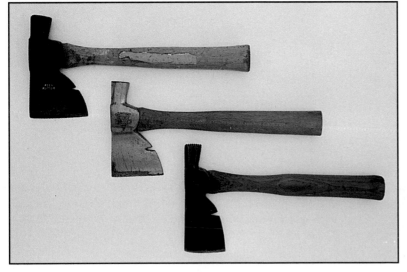

Top: 3¾" lathing hatchet with just Keen Kutter written out which is unusual, $45.00 – 50.00. Middle: E. C. Simmons 3¼" chrome half hatchet, $50.00 – 70.00. Bottom: 2½" E. C. Simmons lathing hatchet with checkered face, $35.00 – 45.00.

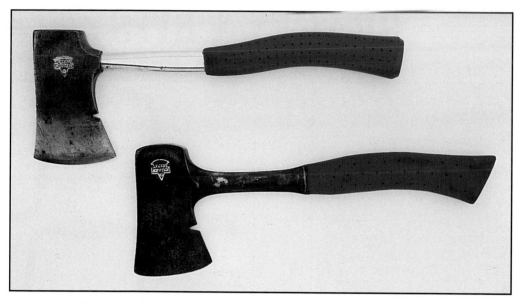

Scout axes, steel shanks with red rubber handles, $40.00 – 55.00.

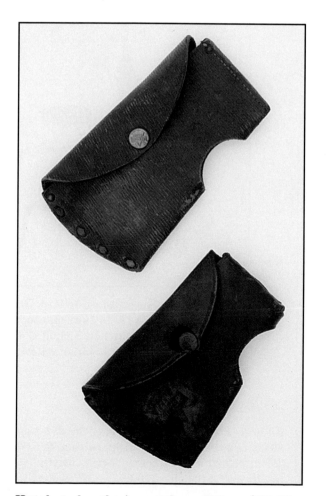

Hatchet gauge, No. S20,
$75.00 – 100.00.

Hatchet sheaths in good condition, $75.00 –
100.00.

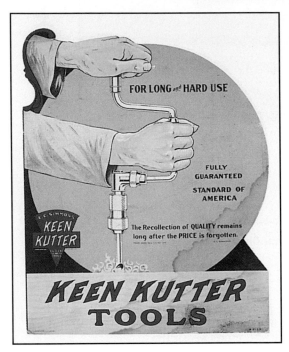

Cardboard self-standing advertisement for Keen Kutter tools showing a brace, 17½" x 14", $300.00 – 400.00.

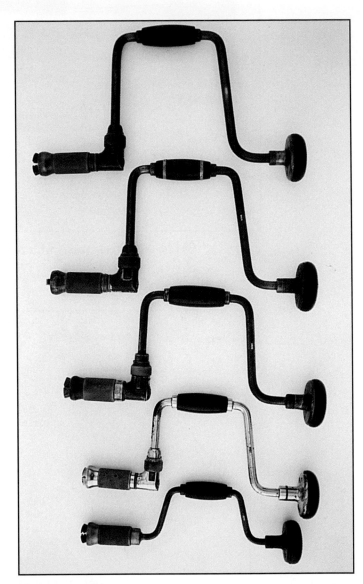

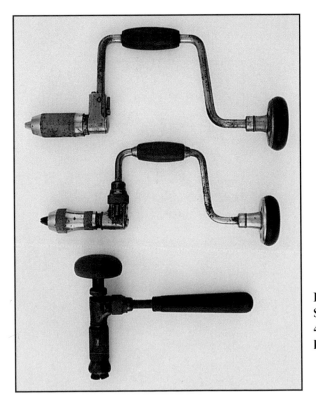

Bit braces. Top to bottom: #KR16, 16" sweep, ratchet, $40.00 – 50.00; #KA14, 14" sweep, ratchet, $35.00 – 45.00; #KA12 12" sweep, ratchet, $35.00 – 45.00; #KR10, 10" sweep, ratchet, $35.00 – 45.00; #KP6, 6" sweep, plain, $75.00 – 100.00.

Bit braces: #K110 N 10" sweep, enclosed ratchet, $35.00 – 45.00; #K18 8" sweep, ratchet, $35.00 – 45.00; #K400 ratchet corner brace, height 7⅜", length 9¾", $100.00 – 150.00.

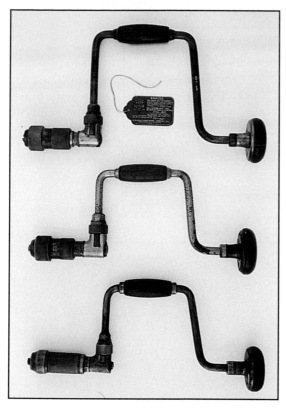

Bit braces: #KBB14 14" sweep, ratchet, $35.00 – 45.00; tag for braces, $50.00 – 75.00; #K710 10" sweep, ratchet, $35.00 – 45.00; #KBC10 10" sweep, ratchet, $35.00 – 45.00.

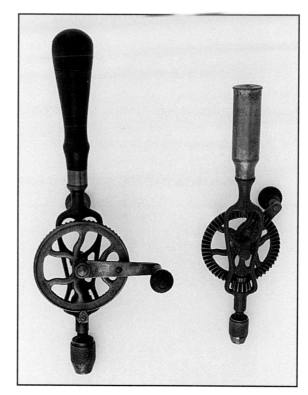

Hand drills: Wooden handle with removable top to hold twist bits, 3½" gear wheel, $75.00 – 125.00. Hollow brass handles holds fluted drill points or any twist drills, revolving cap with separate index compartments, 3⅛" gear wheel, $75.00 – 125.00.

Breast drill with large gear wheel, 5" diameter, 16½" overall length, $75.00 – 125.00.

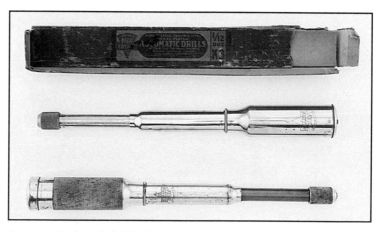

Automatic hand drills, both have patent date Nov. 17, 1891, overall length 9½", contain 8 drill points, $50.00 – 75.00 each. Part of original box the K3 (middle) came in, $10.00 – 15.00 for this condition.

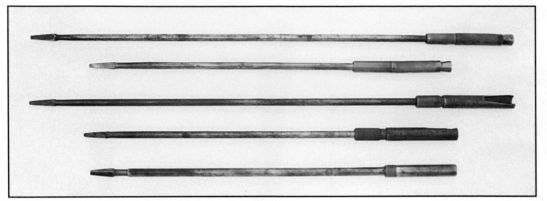

Straight bit extensions, some with patent applied for and some with patent date 3-10-25, sizes 18" and 24" overall, $35.00 – 50.00 each.

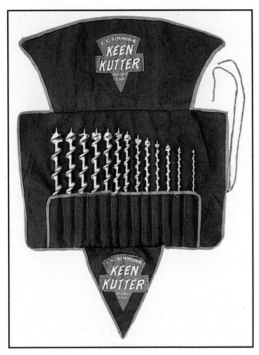

Canvas double emblem auger bit holder, shaped like the emblem, complete with 13 bits, $300.00 – 350.00.

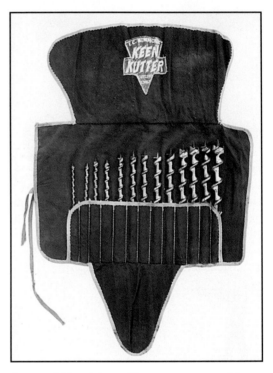

Auger bit set in roll-up canvas emblem-shaped pouch with 13 bits, $225.00 – 275.00.

Auger bit set in plastic roll pouch #KSR13 containing 13 bits from sizes $^4/_{16}$" to $^{16}/_{16}$", $100.00 – 125.00.

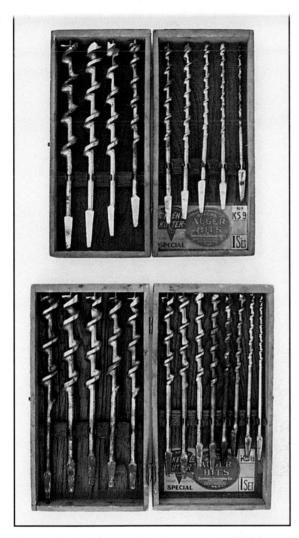

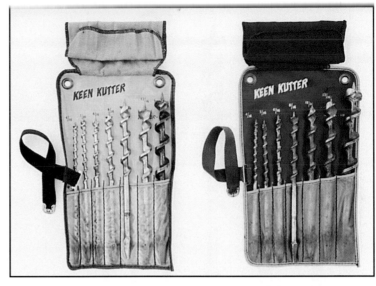

Auger bit sets in plastic roll pouches, both # KSR116 bits range from ⁴⁄₁₆'' to ¹⁴⁄₁₆'', $90.00 – 100.00 each.

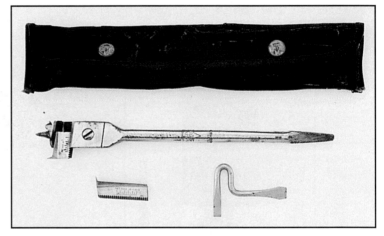

Expansive bit in black leatherette case with emblem buttons, complete with a double-end screwdriver, patent date March 18, 1913. Has two cutter sizes, ⅞'' to 3'', $75.00 – 100.00.

Auger bit sets in wooden boxes. Top: #KS9 contains sizes 4, 5, 6, 7, 8, 10, 12, 14, 16, $115.00 – 125.00 Bottom: #KS13 contains sizes 4 through 16, $125.00 – 175.00.

Expansive bit in original box with two cutters, ⅞'' to 3'', $60.00 – 75.00; expansive bit with one cutter, ⅞'' to 1¾'', no box, "Keen Kutter" written out on it, $20.00 – 25.00.

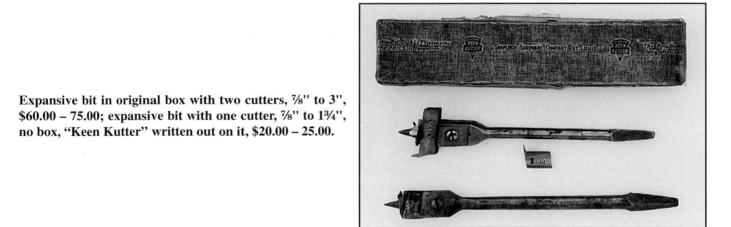

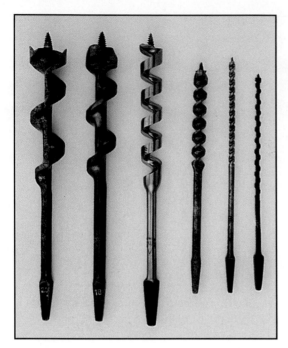

Auger bits, sizes 20, 18, 13, 8, and 3, $7.00 – 12.00 each.

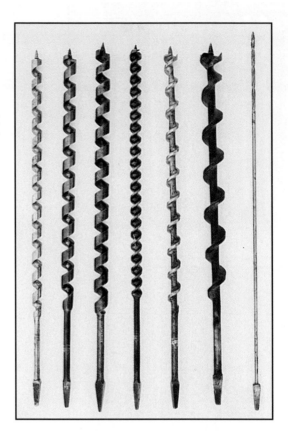

Left to right: Ship car bits, all 16½" length, sizes 9, 11, and 12, $8.00 – 12.00 each. Car bits, all 16½" length sizes, 9, 11, 17, $8.00 – 12.00 each. Wood bit for brace, 18" length, size 6, $8.00 – 12.00.

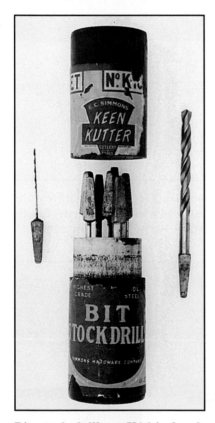

Bit stock drill set K16 in hard-wood cylindrical box containing one each, sizes 2, 3, 4, 5, 6, 7, 8, 10, 12, $175.00 – 225.00; bit value individual, $5.00 – 7.00 each.

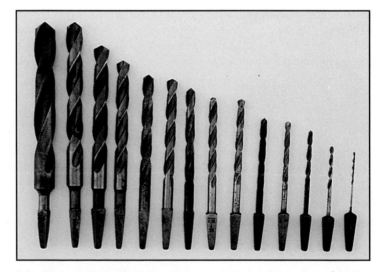

Bit stock twist drills for metal or wood, various sizes, $5.00 – 7.00 each.

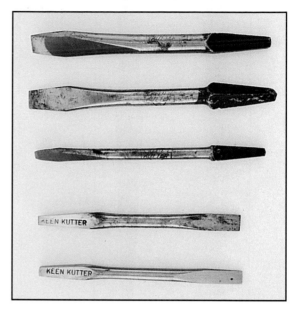

Electrician or bell hangers, bits sizes 16, 12, 10, 8, 6, $8.00 – 12.00 each.

Gimlet bits, single cut to fit a brace, sizes 5, 7, 9, 12, $7.00 – 9.00 each.

Top three: Set of screwdriver bits, sizes ½'', ⅜'', and ⁵⁄₁₆'', $35.00 – 45.00 set. Bottom two: Screwdriver bits, sizes ⁵⁄₁₆'' and ¼'', $8.00 – 12.00 each.

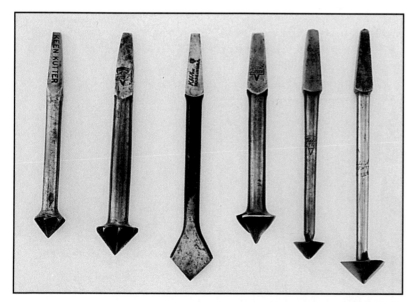

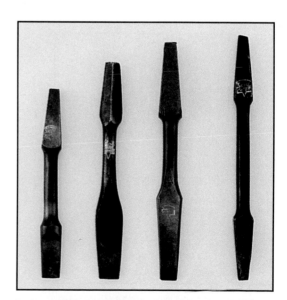

Countersink bits, some for wood and some for metal, $15.00 – 30.00 each.

Left to right: Screwdriver bits, three different, $10.00 – 15.00 each. Screwdriver bit K106 for a brace, points ¼'' and ⁵⁄₁₆'', overall 5'' length, double ended, $50.00 – 75.00.

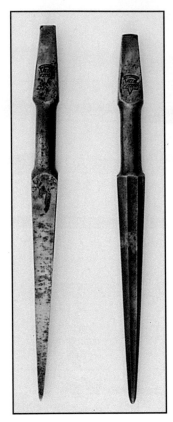

Reamers for wood, both sizes 7⁄16". #K115 square blade, $40.00 – 50.00; #K117 octagonal blade, $40.00 – 50.00.

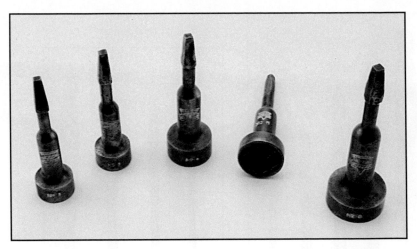

Nut drivers for a brace, sizes No. 1, 3, 4, 5, 8, $25.00 – 30.00 each.

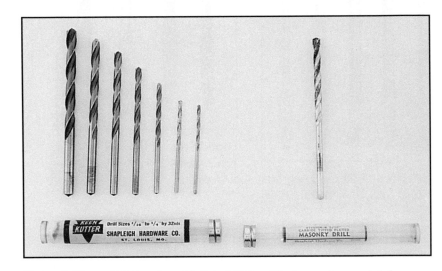

Twist drill set, 7 bits, sizes 1⁄16" to 1⁄4" by 32nds, and round tube container, $70.00 – 90.00 set. Masonry drill F7737GK-K, size 3⁄16" in round tube container, $30.00 – 50.00 set.

Masonry drill set No. F7744GK, containing 1⁄4", 5⁄16", 3⁄8", and 1⁄2" in pouch, $100.00 – 125.00. Each bit has "Keen Kutter" written out on it.

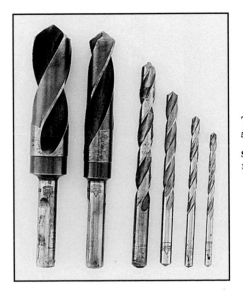

Twist drills, sizes 1", 3⁄4", 13⁄32", 5⁄16", 15⁄64", and 3⁄16". Small sizes, $8.00 – 10.00 each. Over 1⁄2" sizes, $10.00 – 15.00 each.

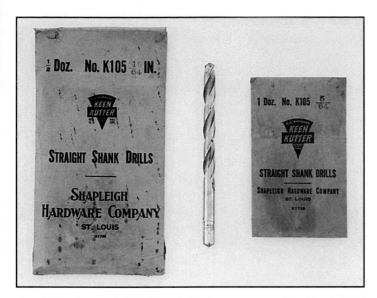

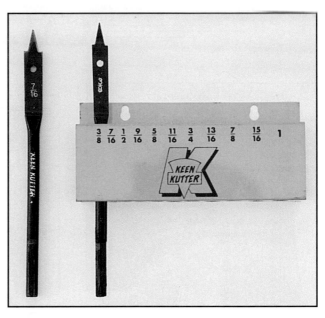

Straight shank drills in original wrappers. Six No. K105 ¹⁹⁄₆₄'', $30.00 – 45.00; one dozen No. K105 ⁵⁄₆₄'', $30.00 – 45.00.

Spade bits, sizes ³⁄₈'' and ⁷⁄₁₆'' for wood, $8.00 – 10.00 each. Wall hung display rack for spade bits, $25.00 – 35.00.

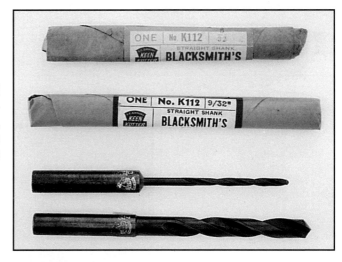

Top to bottom: K112 ⁶⁄₃₂'' Blacksmith's drill in original wrapper with green label, E. C. Simmons, $50.00 – 75.00. K112 ⁹⁄₃₂'' Blacksmith's drill in original wrapper, Shapleigh, $30.00 – 40.00. Blacksmith's drill, also called twist drills, sizes ³⁄₁₆'' and ⁷⁄₁₆'', $10.00 – 15.00 each.

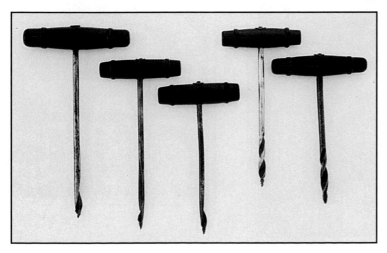

Gimlets, blade extends through handle, three are single cut and two are double cut, $30.00 – 35.00 each.

CALENDARS

Left: Calendar, 1936, saws and squares make up the design and also advertisement for Knop Hardware, $225.00 – 275.00.

Right: Calendar, 1938, advertising 70 years of Keen Kutter Shear Satisfaction and also Trout & Matthias Hardware Co., $150.00 – 175.00.

Left: Calendar, 1940, scissors advertisement as well as Scott Hardware Co., $200.00 – 250.00.

Right: Calendar, 1945, Shawneetown Merc. Company, $150.00 – 175.00.

Left:
Calendar, 1950, "The Future Champion" scene, $150.00 – 175.00.

Right:
Calendar, 1955, Silvery Splendor scene, $150.00 – 175.00.

Calendars, tin, pad type with hardware store name and location. These with the Indian and Capitol Building are more unusual. $125.00 – 175.00 each.

Calendars, tin, pad type with hardware store name and location on it. $75.00 – 125.00 each.

CATALOGS

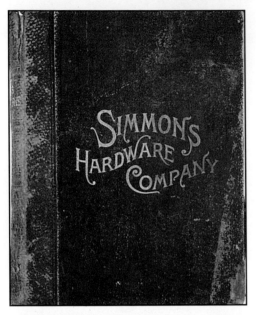

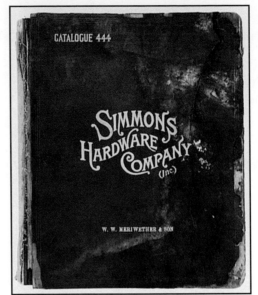

1903 Catalog No. 444, hard leather cover with hardware store name on cover, 2,164 pages in addition to index and information, $250.00 – 350.00 excellent condition.

Jan. 20, 1899 catalog, leather bound containing 1,768 pages with index. Statistics: 4" thick, 16 lbs., 8,350 illustrations. 12,000 copies were printed, using six carloads of paper, 13½ tons tar boards, 11,000 sq. ft. leather, and 24,000 sq. yds. cloth. Binding took 14 months, and it was shipped in 650 cases, forming 110 wagon loads. $900.00 – 1,200.00.

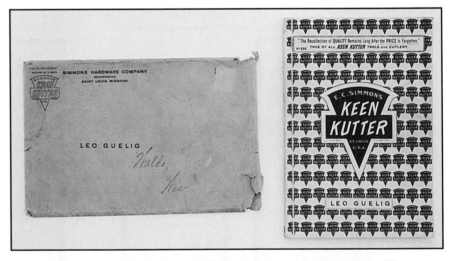

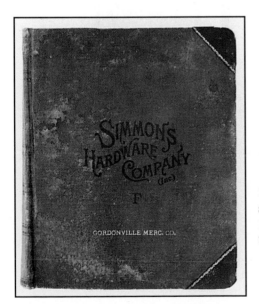

Salesman's catalog containing nothing but Keen Kutter items. The cover and its manila folder have the salesman's name on them. The size of the catalog is 6" x 9" and contains 104 pages, $450.00 – 550.00.

1903 Simmons Hardware Co. F catalog with hardware store's name embossed in gold on cover, leather corners, 1,400 numbered pages in addition to index and information, $400.00 – 600.00.

Left:
1913 Simmons Year Book, Catalog No. K, paper cover, 2,826 numbered pages in addition to index and information, $500.00 – 750.00.

Right:
1921 – 1922 Catalog No. R, paper cover, 2,738 numbered pages in addition to an index and information, $500.00 – 750.00.

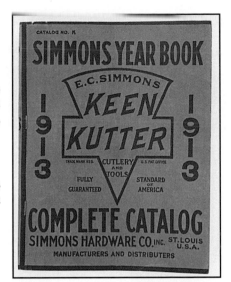

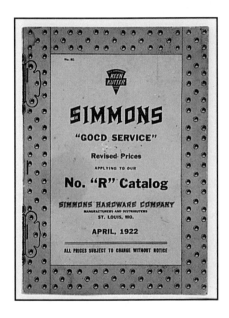

Left:
1922 No. R1 Catalog, 153 pages, revised prices to the R catalog of 1921 – 1922, $100.00 – 125.00.

Right:
1935 Catalog No. V, cloth cover, 2,118 numbered pages in addition to index and information, $325.00 – 425.00.

Left:
1930 Catalog No. U, paper cover, 2,080 numbered pages in addition to index and information, $350.00 – 450.00.

Right:
1939 Catalog No. Z, 2,716 pages, 4½" thick, $300.00 – 400.00.

1942 Shapleigh catalog, Keen Kutter and Diamond Edge, 29 sections, 4" thick, $250.00 – 350.00.

Specialty Catalogs: 1952, No. 478 Farm & Garden Tools, $65.00 – 85.00; 1951, No. 476 Tool Catalog, $65.00 – 85.00; 1951, No. 477 House Furnishing Goods, $65.00 – 85.00; 1949, No. 450 Builders' Hardware, $65.00 – 85.00; 1950 No. 475 Spring & Summer Sporting Goods, $65.00 – 85.00.

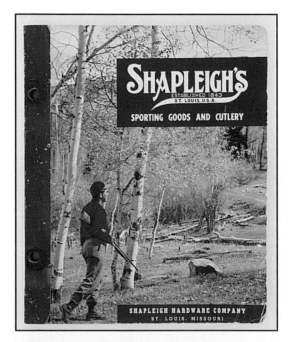

1953 Sporting Goods & Cutlery No. 479. This was probably the replacement for the 1950, No. 475, $65.00 – 85.00.

Shapleigh Hardware Co. SNAPS 1956 Catalog, leather cover, pages numbered to tie in with general catalog pages where similar type of product is shown, $100.00 – 150.00.

Catalog, 1957 Shapleigh, 30 sections, red leather cover with carrying handles, $375.00 – 475.00.

Salesman's catalog carrying case, 15" x 14" x 8½" for carrying catalogs and sales literature to hardware stores, $100.00 – 125.00.

Left:
Repair Parts Catalog, not dated, 85 pages with page numbering from 3001 to 3086, $125.00 – 175.00.

Right:
1911 "The Window Display Manual," 271 numbered pages containing descriptions and photos of various hardware stores' large window displays, several being with Keen Kutter products, $150.00 – 200.00.

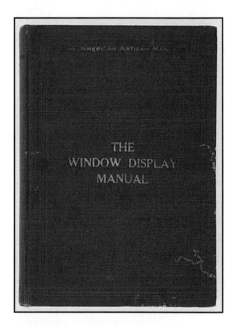

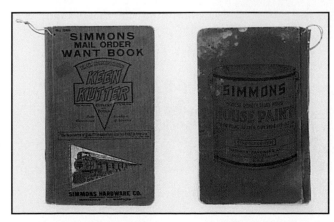

Hardback mail order want book: Back and front view. Front cover is usually the same, but the back can vary with paint cans, lanterns, razors, and advertising items, 6" x 10", $100.00 – 125.00.

Want Books. Left: Winchester-Simmons Co., 6" x 9", $75.00 – 100.00; Right: Simmons, 6" x 9", $50.00 – 75.00.

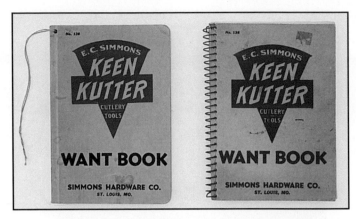

Want Books, yellow. These went along with the 1935 catalog. Hardback, 6½" x 9", $75.00 – 95.00; spiral, 6½" x 9", $50.00 – 75.00.

Shapleigh's Want Books, all spiral. DE & KK 8¾" x 4¾", $30.00 – 50.00. 9¾" x 6½", 1941, $30.00 – 50.00. 9¾" x 6½", Shapleigh on inside, $30.00 – 40.00.

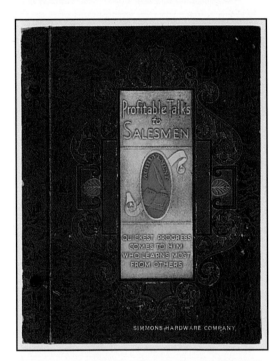

Salesman's incentive book, *Profitable Talks To Salesmen,* 1933, contains bulletins mostly typed on Keen Kutter stationery received in 1933 outlining the "Sales Plan," $275.00 – 325.00.

Salesman's incentive books, "How To Sell" from early 1900s, $50.00 – 75.00.

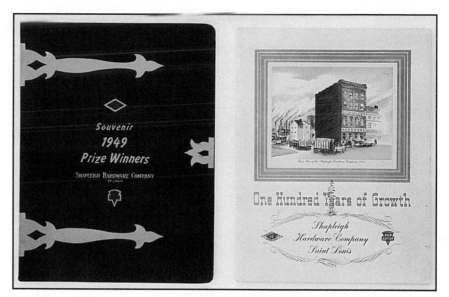

1949 Prize Winners, $125.00 – 175.00; *One Hundred Years of Growth,* $125.00 – 175.00.

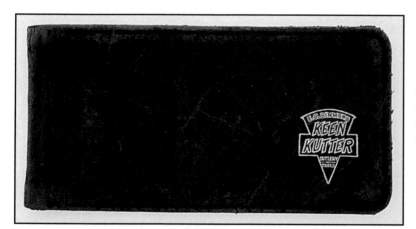

Salesman's note book with 1912 pocket calendar, contains graph paper and pictures of products. Each blank page has Keen Kutter emblem on it, $90.00 – 100.00.

Authors' previous price guides: white, published in 1984; yellow, published in 1990 with updates in 1993 and 1996.

CHISELS & PUNCHES

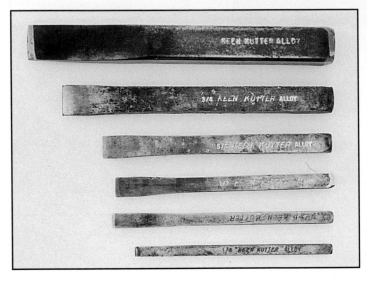

Cold chisels, alloy steel, sizes 1", ¾", ⅝", ½", ⅜", ¼", $10.00 – 20.00 each.

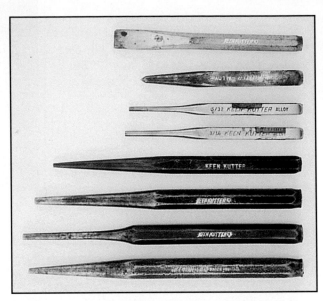

Punches, various sizes, Shapleigh, $10.00 – 20.00 each.

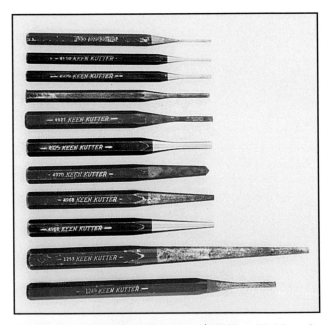

Machine punches, various sizes, $10.00 – 20.00 each. These were some of the last ones made by Shapleigh. Val-Test later distributed the remaining stock and also produced some with Keen Kutter written out following the same numbering system.

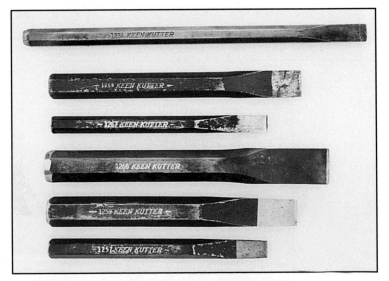

Cold chisels, various sizes, $10.00 – 20.00 each. Some of the last ones Shapleigh made. Val-Test later distributed the remaining stock and also produced some with Keen Kutter written out following the same numbering system.

Cape chisels, steel, three different sizes, $15.00 – 25.00 each.

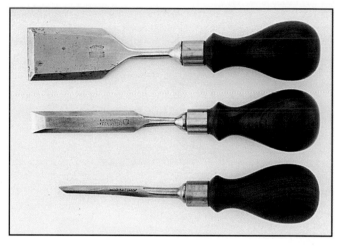

Butt chisels, tanged beveled edge with rosewood handles, sizes 1½'', ⅝'', ¼'', $50.00 – 75.00 each.

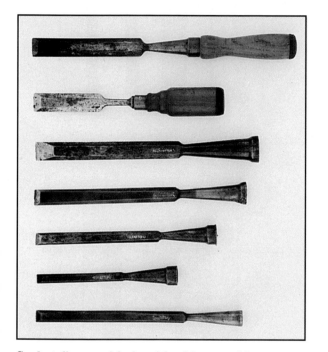

Socket firmer chisels with older markings, most have reinforced shoulders, $10.00 – 25.00 each.

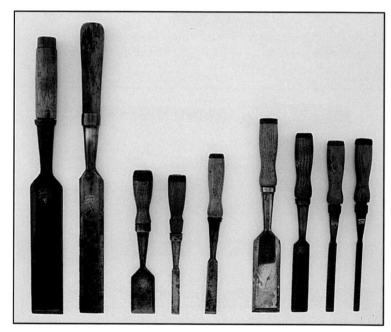

Firmer chisels with reinforced shoulders: 2'', very heavy beveled edges, unusual, $25.00 – 45.00; 1½'', beveled edges, $20.00 – 30.00; 1½'', butt chisel beveled edges, $10.00 – 15.00; ½'', butt chisel beveled edges, $10.00 – 15.00; ¾'', plain back socket firmer, $10.00 – 15.00; four socket firmers, beveled edges, sizes 1¾'', 1'', ½'', ⅜'', $10.00 – 20.00 each.

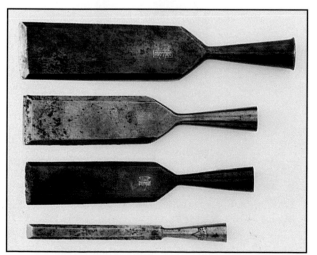

Socket firmer chisels with beveled edges, sizes 2'', 1¼'', 1½'', ½'', $10.00 – 25.00 each.

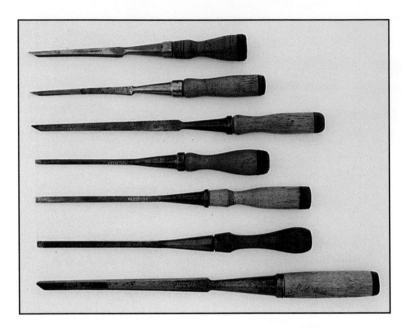

Mortising chisels, narrow with thick blade used for cutting a deep mortise, sizes ⅛", ³⁄₁₆", ⅜", ¼", $10.00 – 25.00 each.

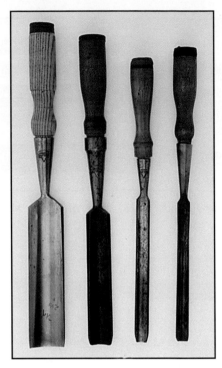

Gouges, handled socket firmer, sizes ½", ⅝", 1", 1½", $35.00 – 60.00 each.

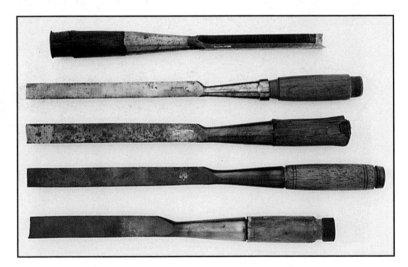

Socket corner chisels with heavy steel ferrules at top, sizes ¾", ⅞", 1", $30.00 – 50.00 each.

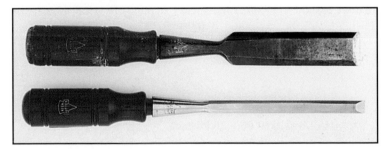

Socket firmer chisels with red tenite plastic handles, beveled edge, sizes 1" and ⅜", $10.00 – 15.00 each.

Odd chisel, no handle, size 1½", $10.00 – 15.00. Wood chisel No. 1671, all purpose steel, 1½" x 7" long with upset head. Can be used with any type hammer. Has part of its paper label, $15.00 – 20.00.

Cardboard box that K45 socket butt chisel handles came in, $25.00 – 35.00; handles, $5.00 – 7.00 each.

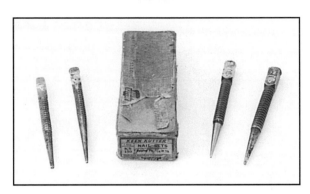

Nail set, various types, $8.00 – 12.00 each; nail set box that one dozen KS150 assorted sets came in, $15.00 – 20.00.

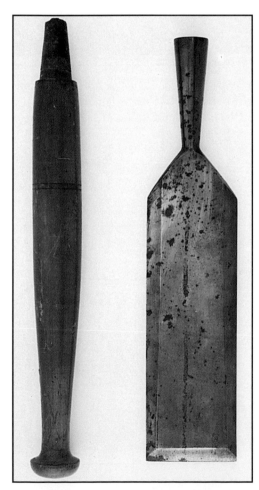

Slick, has wooden handle, beveled edge, blade length 16", width 3½", $300.00 – 400.00.

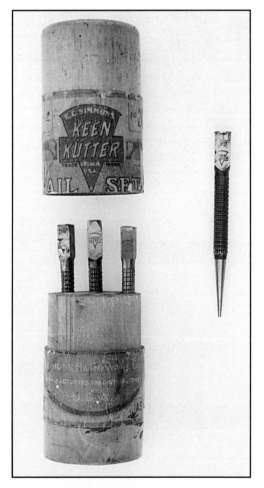

Nail set K200 in round barrel, one dozen assorted sizes came in container of assorted sizes, $\frac{1}{32}$, $\frac{2}{32}$, $\frac{3}{32}$, $\frac{4}{32}$. Value of container alone, $175.00 – 225.00; value of nail set, $8.00 – 12.00 each.

DISPLAYS

Tool window display No. 216, lithographed cut-out, 40" high and 56" wide, made in the three panel effect. With it are cardboard emblems, cardboard sign, brochure explaining how to display it, and trade card (unused) telling dealer date display is to be used for "Keen Kutter Week," $2,500.00 – 3,000.00.

Butcher knife display, 23½" x 14", stand-up easel type, cardboard bull. Still has the original "How to Care For" tag on back. Display without knife, $1,200.00 – 1,500.00.

Kitchen knife display stand, wooden, 18" long, 12" high, mahogany finish, slotted top to insert butcher knives and slicers, cork filled bottom to display paring knives, $300.00 – 350.00.

Butcher knife window or counter display, easel back cardboard shaped like a lamb. Overall size, 18¼" x 14½", furnished free with an assortment of butcher knives, slicers, etc. of over $75.00 or more, $1,200.00 – 1,500.00.

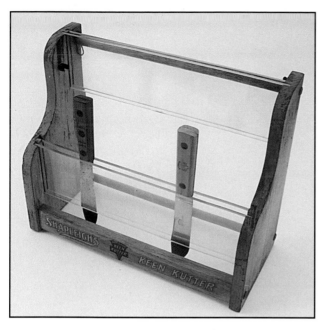

Knife display for kitchen knives, 13¼" tall, 16" wide, 7" depth, $100.00 – 150.00.

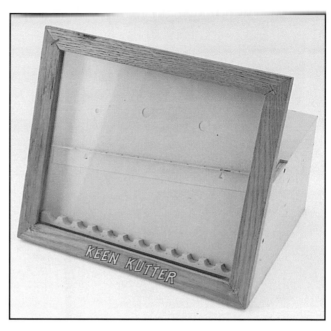

Kitchen knife and scissor display case, 10¼" deep, 13½" wide, 12" tall, slant front. It has a lift-up lid and large storage area inside, $75.00 – 125.00.

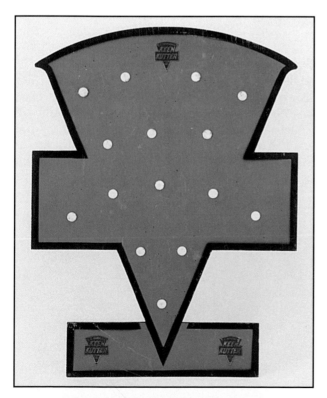

Scissor display counter board, emblem-shaped, easel back, wooden, $100.00 – 175.00.

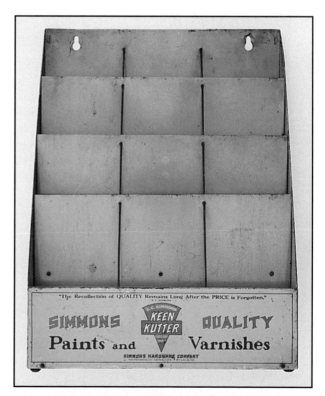

Paint rack, color card holder No. 275, tin, 15¼" high, 11¼" wide, 4¾" deep, $250.00 – 375.00.

Paint rack, three tiers, 33" tall x 26" wide. As is, $350.00 – 400.00; good condition, $700.00 – 750.00.

Tire display holder, metal, 12¾" x 7¼", folds down to a flat position of 22". Mfg. by Doering Bros. Cin. OH Pat No. 1,284,260, $350.00 – 400.00.

Left to right: Display boxes with celluloid logo buttons, logos on front, top lifts ½" for slant display, storage area inside. 10½" x 3½", felt lined, for table cutlery, $50.00 – 75.00; 9" x 4", felt lined, for shears, $50.00 – 75.00; 7" x 2¾" felt lined, for pocket knives, $50.00 – 75.00; 4½" x 2¾" sunk top for two pocket knives, $30.00 – 50.00; 4½" x 2½" colorful, tape lift, pocket knives, $30.00 – 50.00; 4½" x 2½" colorful, Celebrated pocket knives, $25.00 – 45.00.

Easel type metal display rack, display area 22" x 28½", overall height 4'2", $200.00 – 250.00.

Chisel and punch display stands, logo design, two different sizes. One has 17 holes and is 6" x 8" x 1¾" thick. The other has 24 holes and is 5" x 6½" x 1¾" thick and held nail sets. They are both Shapleigh, $90.00 – 115.00 each.

Paper holder, double rack, 18" top and 24" bottom, with string holder attachment, $250.00 – 325.00.

Paper holder with 12" wide roll of paper, 12" tall x 17" across top. Feet are logo-shaped cast iron. Paper holder, $150.00 – 175.00; roll of paper, $475.00 – 650.00.

Tool display rack, 4' 10" wide x 2' 4" tall. Each tool has the number and outline listed, $175.00 – 200.00.

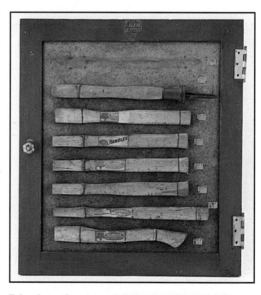

Display doors with tools used on large wooden enclosed showcases. 23" wide x 26" tall door containing hammer handles. Door only, $55.00 – 75.00. 23" wide x 46" tall door (not pictured), $65.00 – 85.00.

Keen Kutter and Diamond Edge, 30" x 50" framed picture showing what Schlitt Hardware looked like in June, 1944 (left side) compared to being remodeled by the Store Modernization Department of Shapleigh Hardware (right side), $800.00 – 1,000.00.

Small brass emblem used on tool boxes and various displays, $50.00.

ELECTRICAL TOOLS

Wooden tool rack for electric tools, 31" wide x 28" high, $175.00 – 225.00.

Skill or clutch saws, both 7", one KK70, other KK258GK, $45.00 – 65.00 each.

Circular saw blades: 5⅞" combination with original sleeve, $65.00 – 95.00; 8" combination rip with original sleeve, $65.00 – 95.00.

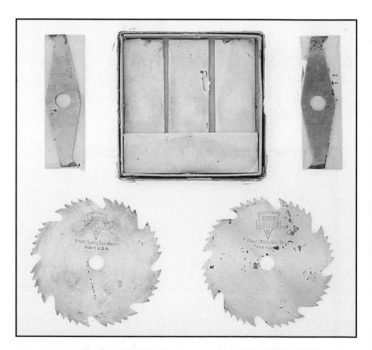

Dado saw blades, 5½" diameter, has outside cutters and inside cutters, $75.00 – 100.00.

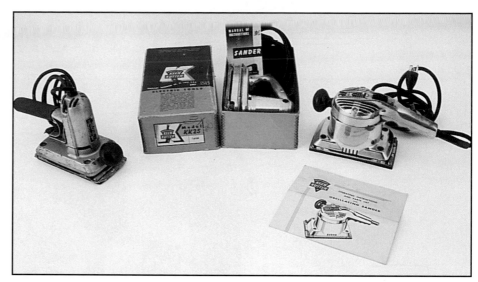

Electric sanders. Left: KK250B oscillating sander, $40.00 – 50.00. Center: KK25 with original box and papers, mint condition, $100.00 – 150.00. Right: KK242 with booklet, $75.00 – 100.00.

KK243B ¼'' drill, came with a sanding pad and drill bits. Complete, $100.00 – 150.00. KK200 ¼'' drill, $45.00 – 50.00.

Electric hedge trimmer, KK57, $45.00 – 55.00. Electric bench grinder KK50, $45.00 – 55.00. Electric jig saw KK249, $45.00 – 55.00.

FARM TOOLS

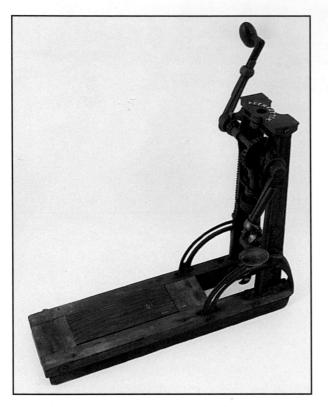

Left:
Boring machine with calibrated frame, "Keen Kutter" is written on top of metal frame, $275.00 – 350.00.

Right:
Post drill #K1902, $175.00 – 225.00.

KM400 machinist's vise, stationary base, $175.00 – 225.00. KS312 machinist's vise, swivel base, $200.00 – 250.00.

Vise, combination pipe swivel base, KC/412, $225.00 – 275.00.

Hand-powdered grinders. Left: Sickle and tool grinder, $65.00 – 85.00. Right: Small tool grinder, $75.00 – 100.00.

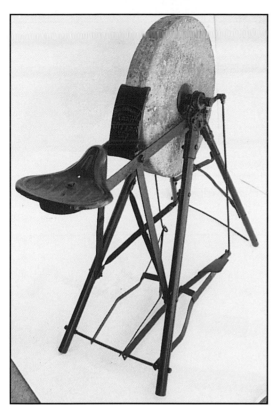

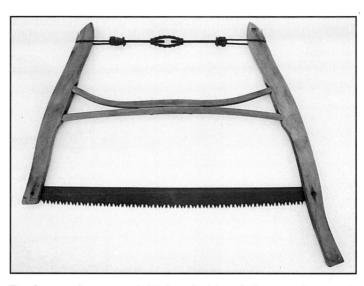

Buck saw, logo on right hand side of the wooden part, $85.00 – 100.00.

Grindstone, sit-down style, $100.00 – 150.00.

Spoke pointers, two different sizes, $70.00 – 80.00.

One-man cross-cut saw #309 with emblem on blade, $150.00 – 200.00.

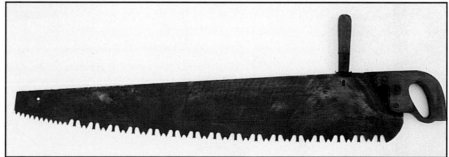

Two-man saw, $125.00 – 175.00.

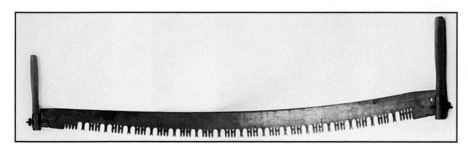

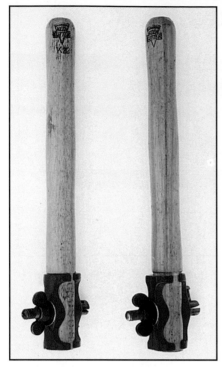

Cross-cut saw handles, overall length 13¾", $50.00 – 75.00 pair.

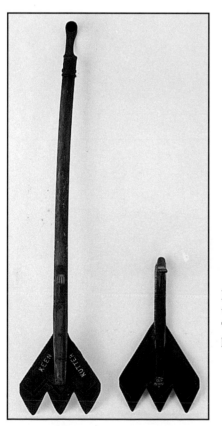

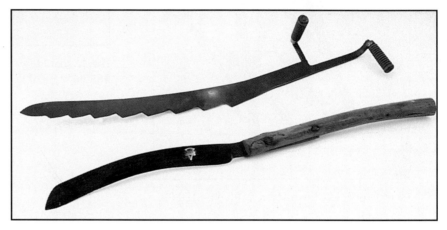

Dehorning saw, cast iron with wooden handle, $65.00 – 85.00.

Hay knife with serrated edges, $75.00 – 100.00. Hedge knife, wooden handle, $40.00 – 60.00.

Farrier's knife, bone handle, $75.00 – 100.00.

Hay knives, two different, one with logo and one with Keen Kutter written out, $75.00 – 100.00 each. These are priced for good condition. Note the one has a broken handle.

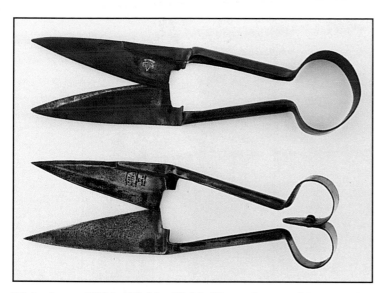

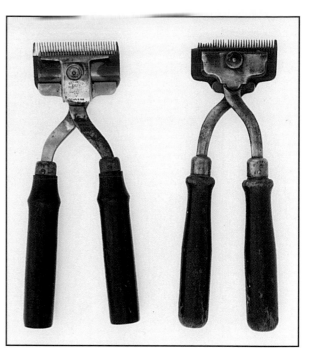

Mule shears K100, $20.00 – 30.00; Sheep shears with engraving of man shearing sheep, marked "Made In England", $100.00 – 125.00.

Horse clippers, 10½" long, K940 and K920, $50.00 – 75.00 each.

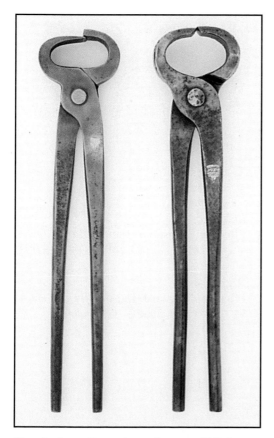

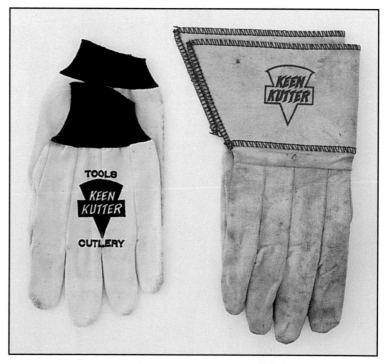

Farrier's nail cutting pincers, 12" (over-laps), $30.00 – 40.00. Blacksmith's shoeing pincers, 12", $30.00 – 40.00.

Left: Cotton gloves advertising cutlery, $50.00 – 75.00. Right: Gauntlet-style gloves, $75.00 – 100.00.

FILES

Cardboard file boxes, for 10" mill bastard file F6589GK, twelve to a box, $25.00 – 35.00; 6" slim taper file, KCSS6, twelve to a box, $25.00 – 35.00.

File handles with steel ferrules, $25.00 – 35.00 each.

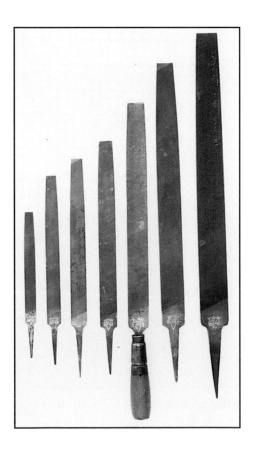

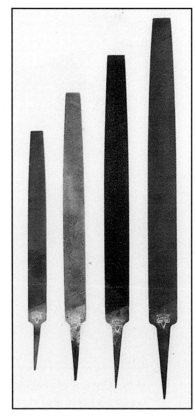

Left:
Files, mill bastard, flat single cut, sizes 6", 8", 9", 10", 12", 14", 16", $8.00 – 15.00 each.

Right:
Files, mill bastard, flat double cut, sizes 10", 12", 14", 16", $8.00 – 15.00 each.

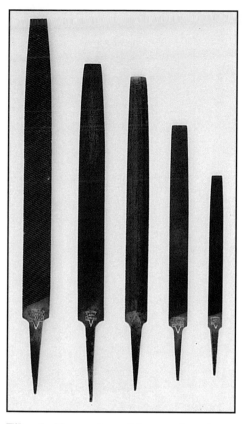

Files, half-round used by woodworkers, sizes 6", 8", 10", 12", $8.00 – 15.00 each.

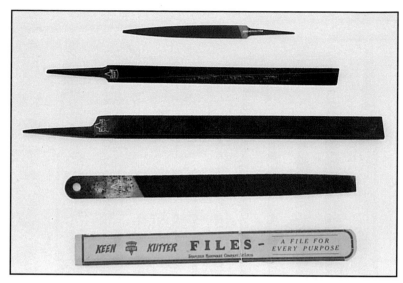

Top to bottom: Warding bastard cut file, 4", used by jewelers, machinists, locksmiths for key notching, $15.00 – 20.00; cant saw file, for cross-cut saw, has M-shaped teeth, 8", $15.00 – 20.00; cross-cut saw file, 10", $15.00 – 20.00; safety file 10", no tang, pocket carrying, $15.00 – 20.00; file holder out of cardboard, $20.00 – 30.00.

Files, taper, designed for filing hand saws, each has Keen Kutter written out, six different, regular, slim, and extra slim, $8.00 – 15.00 each.

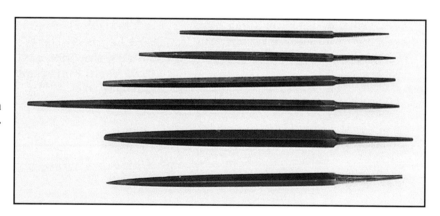

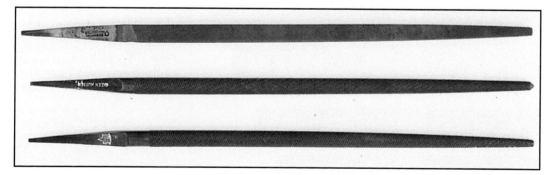

Files, bastard, used in all branches of mechanical industry, each 14" long, one square, two round, $12.00 – 18.00 each.

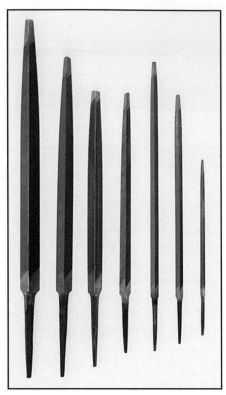

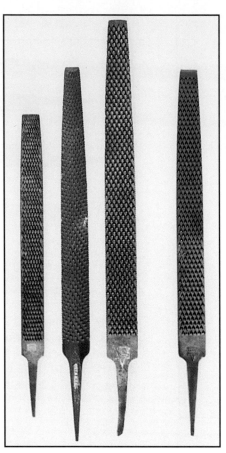

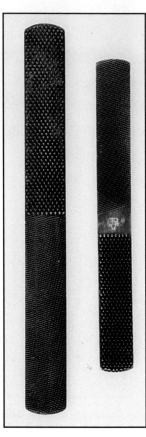

Files, taper, designed for filing hand saws, each with logo, seven different, regular, slim, and extra slim, $8.00 – 15.00 each.

Left to right: Half-round wood rasps, used by wheelwrights and carriage builders, sizes 10", 12", 14", $8.00 – 15.00 each. Flat wood rasps, 12", $8.00 – 15.00.

Shoe rasps, used by shoe-makers, sizes 8", 10", $10.00 – 15.00 each.

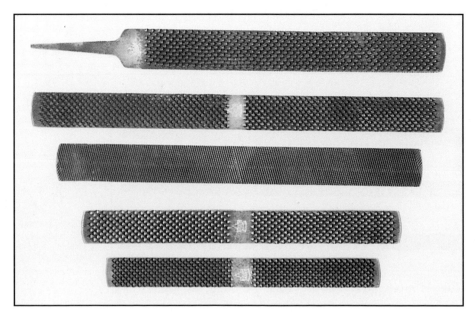

Tanged horse rasp, used by horseshoers, 14", $10.00 – 15.00; plain slim horse rasp, 18", 16", 14", 12", $10.00 – 15.00 each. Horse rasps are always rasps on one side and file on the other.

HAMMERS

E. C. Simmons curved claw, round neck hammers, numbers are written on end of handle. Left to right: 5 oz., #K514, $150.00 – 200.00; 7 oz., #K613 and #KN7, $100.00 – 150.00; 10 oz., #K612½, $35.00 – 55.00; 16 oz., #KN16, $35.00 – 55.00; 25 oz., $35.00 – 55.00.

E. C. Simmons hexagon neck curved claw hammers. 16 oz., $35.00 – 55.00; 7 oz., $100.00 – 150.00.

Left:
E. C. Simmons dynamic hexagon head and curved claw hammers, sizes 16 oz. and 13 oz., $40.00 – 55.00. These hammers were dynamically balanced for greater power in both driving and pulling.

Right:
Left to right: Ladies' hammer, 3¼" head, overall 10¾", $75.00 – 125.00; E. C. Simmons Blue Brand hammer, stamped on one side and etched on other, $75.00 – 100.00; E. C. Simmons chrome K3 nail hammer, $75.00 – 100.00.

Shapleigh hexagon neck curved claw hammers. Left to right: 16 oz. with paper label on handle, $75.00 – 100.00; 13 oz., $40.00 – 50.00; 7 oz., $100.00 – 150.00.

Shapleigh hammers, steel shank, rubber handles, hexagon necks. Left to right: 20 oz. straight claw; two 16 oz. curved claw with different type shanks. $35.00 – 45.00 each.

This is a mint machinist's riveting KPRO 4 oz. hammer with label on handle, $200.00 – 250.00; this hammer in normal used condition would be $35.00 – 45.00.

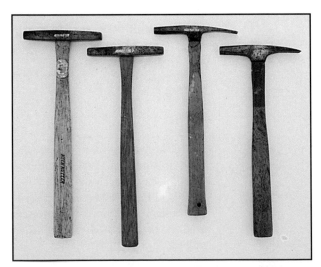

Magnetic tack hammers. Left: with original sticker label, $150.00 – 200.00. Second: regular, $30.00 – 40.00; two on right with claws, $30.00 – 40.00 each.

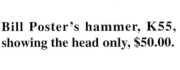

Bill Poster's hammer, K55, showing the head only, $50.00.

Left: Two machinist riveting hammers, $30.00 – 35.00 each. Right: Tinner's riveting hammer, $30.00 – 35.00.

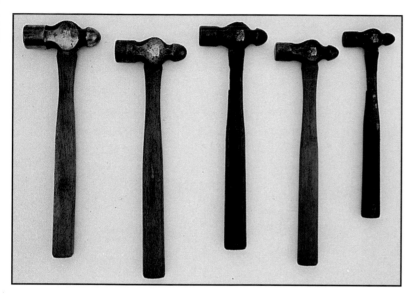

Shapleigh ball-pein hammers, 32 oz., 20 oz., 16 oz., 12 oz., 6 oz., $45.00 – 90.00 each.

E. C. Simmons ball-pein hammers, 32 oz., 24 oz., 20 oz., 16 oz., $45.00 – 85.00 each.

E. C. Simmons ball-pein hammers. Left to right: 12 oz., 8 oz., 6 oz., 4 oz., $55.00 – 85.00. Original handle, mint finish, $100.00 – 125.00. Right: Jeweler's hammer, $125.00 – 175.00.

Blacksmith-riveters hammers. Top: Straight-pein, $100.00 – 125.00; Center: Cross-pein, $125.00 – 150.00; Bottom: Flat top with hole in top, $75.00 – 100.00.

Shapleigh blacksmith shop hammer, 48 oz. and 40 oz., $50.00 – 65.00.

Blacksmith's hand hammer,
4 lb., $75.00 – 100.00.

E. C. Simmons and Shapleigh brick hammers. First three on
left have head lengths of 8½", 7½", and 6½", $35.00 – 45.00.
Right: 5½" head length, $55.00 – 75.00.

E. C. Simmons blacksmith shop
hammers, 32 oz. and 42 oz., $55.00 –
75.00.

E. C. Simmons bricklayer's
skutch, $125.00 – 175.00.

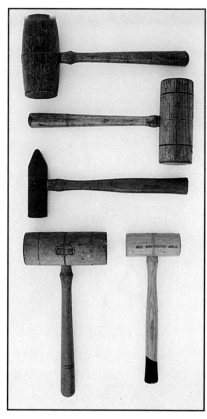

Left: E. C. Simmons chrome farrier's hammer with whale back claw, KF10, 10 oz., $150.00 – 175.00. Right: Two E. C. Simmons farrier's hammers, $75.00 – 100.00 each.

Left: E. C. Simmons shoe cobbler hammer, $125.00 – 175.00. Right: E. C. Simmons prospecting pick, $75.00 – 100.00.

Four wooden mallets; largest has a double Keen Kutter stamp on it, $45.00 – 90.00. Rubber mallet with wooden handle, $45.00 – 90.00.

Saw setting hammer, 7 oz., with original sticker, mint, never used, $200.00 – 250.00. Same hammer with normal use, $40.00 – 60.00.

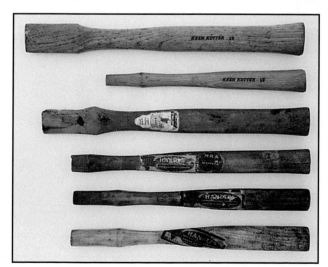

Replacement handles for various hammers, many with part of original labels, $10.00 – 30.00 each.

Food chopper display stand. Wooden pedestal type, 11¾" tall, 14¼" diameter across top. The top is removable. Value without choppers, $300.00 – 400.00.

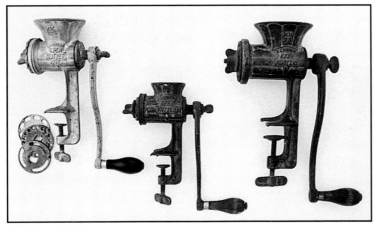

Cookbooks that came with food choppers, $25.00 – 40.00 each.

Food choppers, clamp to table type, K22½ large size, $10.00 – 15.00; K10, small size, $10.00 – 15.00; K23, extra large size, $10.00 – 15.00.

Food choppers in original boxes, $65.00 – 85.00 each; stuffing attachment (only the box is marked), $75.00 – 100.00; cookbook that came with food chopper, $30.00 – 35.00; tag for food chopper, $10.00 – 15.00.

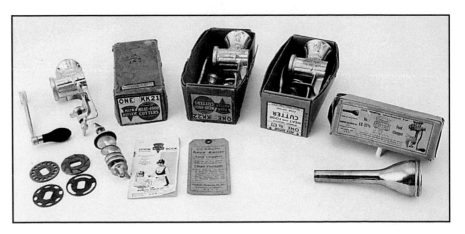

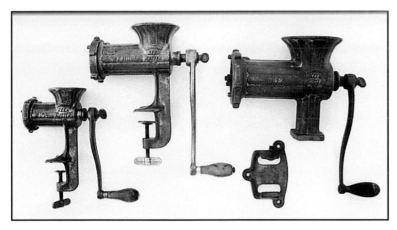

Meat cutter, clamp to table type, K105 family size, $20.00 – 30.00; K110 large family size, $20.00 – 30.00; K112 large family size with separate base plate, sliding base, and thumb screw, $40.00 – 50.00.

Corn mill, clamp to table type, cast iron, patent Aug. 9, '09, $125.00 – 150.00.

Corn mill, S.H. Co. No. 1½ Korn Krusher, cast iron body, hopper, and wheel, $125.00 – 150.00.

Simmons Koffee Krusher No. 12, cast iron, double fly wheels, 8¾" diameter, with drawer, covered hopper, 4 oz. capacity, 12½" overall height. Original color was blue/red/gold, $1,400.00.

S.H. Co., Koffee Krusher, St. Louis, Mo., coffee mill, slide cover and drawer, 4" x 4" hopper, approximately 12½" tall x 5" wide, $400.00 – 500.00.

S.H. Co., Koffee Krusher, No. 10, St. Louis, Mo., coffee mill, clamp-to-table style, open hopper 3½" x 4", approximately 11½" tall x 5½" wide, $225.00 – 300.00.

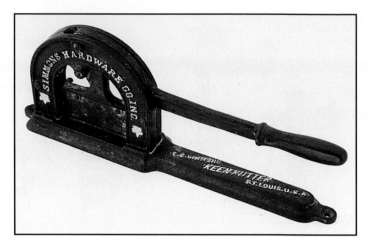

Tobacco cutter, cast iron, $325.00 – 400.00.

Apple parer or peeler, two different styles. They pare the entire apple and eject it, $125.00 – 175.00 each.

Waffle iron, cast iron, four sections with small logo, cake size 6¼", low base type, "Simmons" embossed on the lid, $125.00 – 175.00.

Waffle iron, cast iron with four sections, 7¼" cake size with Keen Kutter logo. The lid has "E. C. Simmons" embossed in it. Low base type. The reproduction was made like this one. $125.00 – 175.00.

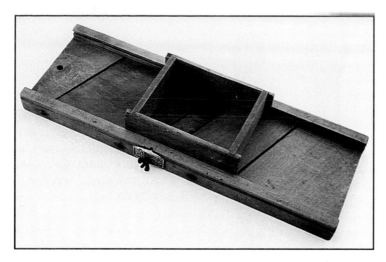

Kraut cutter, single 9" blade, 26¼" length, patent date Oct. 1904, cast iron logo on side and "Keen Kutter" marked on top, $75.00 – 100.00.

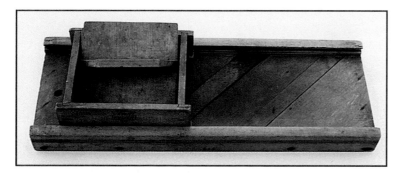

Kraut cutter, single 8" blade, 26½" length, only marking is on the side of the sliding box, $70.00 – 90.00.

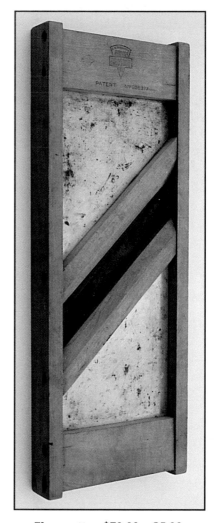

Slaw cutter, $70.00 – 85.00.

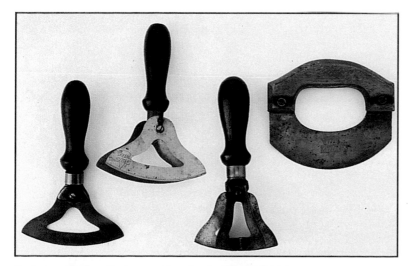

Left to right: mincing knife, single blade, $30.00 – 40.00; mincing knife, double bladed, $30.00 – 40.00; star mincer with six blades, $30.00 – 45.00; KBB mincing knife, single blade, $35.00 – 45.00.

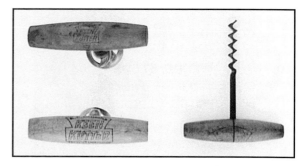

Cork screws, three different styles, $35.00 – 45.00 each.

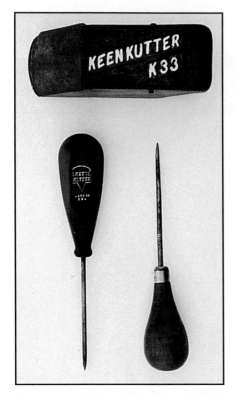

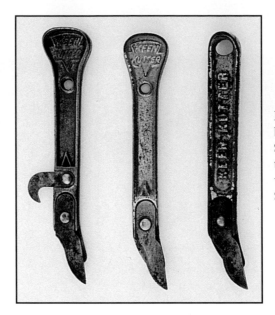

Left to right: Can opener with bottle opener attachment, unusual, $125.00 – 175.00. Can opener, logo type, $20.00 – 25.00. Can opener with "Keen Kutter" written out, $20.00 – 25.00.

Ice shaver K33, $100.00 – 125.00. Ice pick KR15, hard rubber type handle with six flat sides, $75.00 – 100.00. Ice pick, wood handle with brass ferrule and logo and patent date on the iron pick, $100.00 – 125.00.

Bottle stoppers, porcelain, flat side or top reads: Contents 8½'' FL. OZS. Small side reads: Pat'd KKutter Feb/1893, $75.00 – 100.00 each.

Pot holder, size 5¾'' x 5½'', opposite side blank, $75.00 – 100.00.

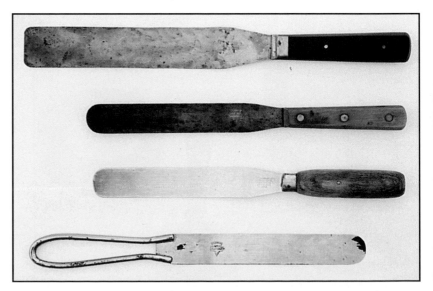

Kitchen spatulas, 9'' blade, $20.00 – 25.00; K366 with 7'' blade, $20.00 – 25.00; 7¼'' blade, $20.00 – 25.00; 7½'' blade all metal, $20.00 – 25.00.

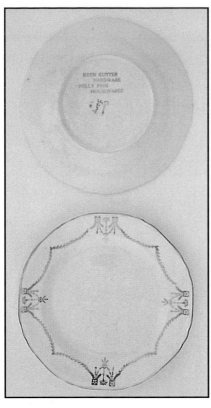

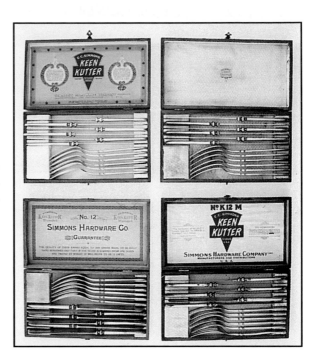

Table cutlery sets, four different sets, silverplate, each with six knives and forks in original wooden boxes, $75.00 – 125.00 each set.

Saucer, Polly Prime Housewares, semi-porcelain chinaware #290 series. Ivory body with dainty chain design, double tracing finish, novelty effect at edges. Each has "Keen Kutter" written on back, $40.00 – 60.00 each.

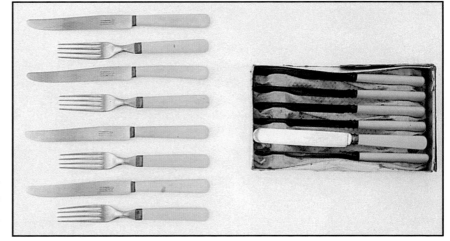

Left: Tableware, 4 forks and knives, yellow celluloid handles, $50.00 set. Right: Butter knives, 6 with celluloid handles, in box, $55.00 – 65.00 set.

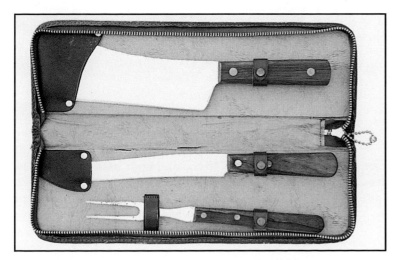

Kitchen cutlery set with leather zipper case marked Keen Kutter on front, $100.00 – 125.00.

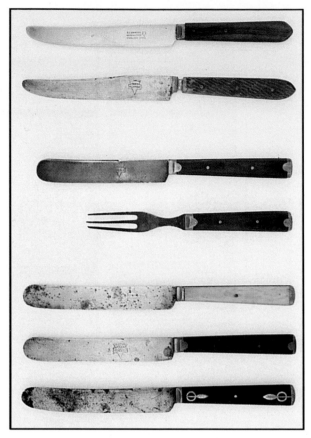

Top to Bottom: K250, cocobola handle steak knife, $10.00; K715 stag handle steak knife, $10.00; 2 pc. set table cutlery with metal bolsters and caps, $15.00 – 20.00; K400 bone handle knife, $10.00; cocobola handle knife, $10.00; knife with fancy metal bolsters and caps, $10.00.

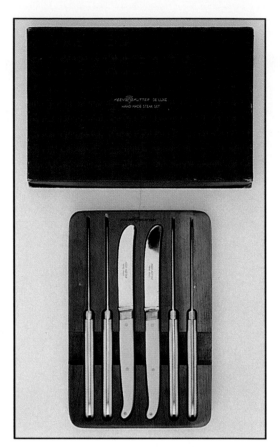

Deluxe steak knife set, handmade, on a wooden board with case, $100.00 – 125.00.

Cardboard box for No. 210 table knives and forks set, $30.00 – 40.00. Cardboard box for K160 butcher knives, box held one-half dozen, $30.00 – 40.00. Butcher knife with 6" blade, K160, $25.00 – 30.00.

Top to bottom: K4612 cooking knife with 12" blade, $20.00 – 30.00; K10 cooking knife with 8" blade, $20.00 – 30.00; K8 butcher knife with 12" blade, $20.00 – 25.00; K160 butcher knife with 7" blade, $15.00 – 20.00; K164 sticking knife with 6" blade, $45.00 – 65.00.

Butcher knives with blade lengths. Top to bottom: 8¼" N622, $10.00 – 15.00; 8¼" hammer forged, $10.00 – 15.00; 8" hollow ground, $15.00 – 20.00; 6", No. 36, $10.00 – 15.00; 6½" metal logo in the handle, $30.00 – 40.00; 5½" logo in handle, $20.00 – 25.00.

Top to bottom: Bread knife with 9½" blade, $20.00 – 25.00; bread knife, serrated edge, 9½" blade, $20.00 – 25.00; K33 lunch slicer 8" blade, Kobalt, $15.00 – 20.00; K37 lunch slicer 9" swagged blade, Kobalt, $15.00 – 20.00; lunch slicer, 8" blade, celluloid handle, $15.00 – 20.00; vegetable knife, all metal, 6" blade, $15.00 – 20.00.

Top to bottom: K52 ham slicing knife 10" blade, $20.00 – 25.00; K8101 pot fork, cocobola handle, $35.00 – 50.00; roast beef butcher's knife, 12" blade, $20.00 – 25.00.

Paring knives with 3" blades, $10.00 – 20.00 each. Bottom two are grapefruit knives, each with serrated double edge curved blades, $25.00 – 30.00 each.

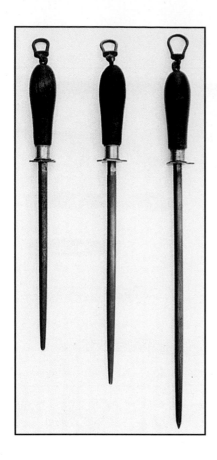

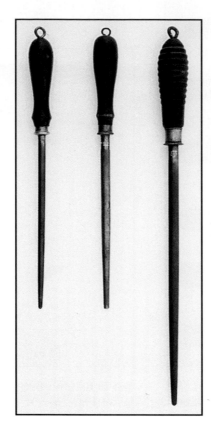

Left:
Knife steels, all have the emblem-shaped guard. Blade sizes 10", 12", 14", $30.00 – 50.00 each.

Right:
Knife steels, 8" blade, $20.00 – 25.00; 8" blade K540-8 marked on it, $15.00 – 20.00; 12" blade, $15.00 – 20.00.

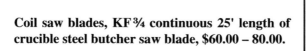

Coil saw blades, KF¾ continuous 25' length of crucible steel butcher saw blade, $60.00 – 80.00.

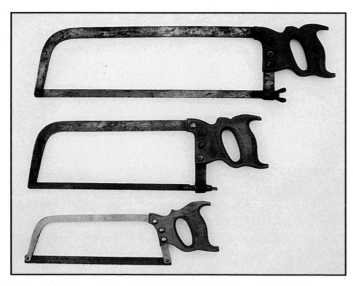

Top: Butcher saw, 20" blade, $35.00 – 50.00. Center: butcher saw, 15" blade, $35.00 – 50.00. Bottom: K2 meat saw, 12" blade, $35.00 – 50.00.

Butcher's chopper with 8" blade, $50.00 – 75.00; household cleaver, 7" blade, $35.00 – 50.00; household cleaver, 6" blade, $25.00 – 40.00.

Carver set, No. 9004, 9" in original box, $150.00 – 200.00.

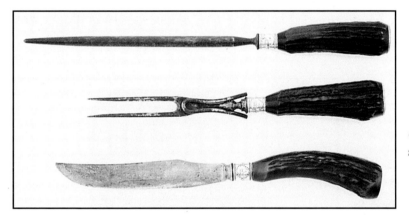

Carving sets, 3-piece, stag handles, sterling silver ferrules, mirror finish, marking only on knife, $50.00 – 55.00 each set.

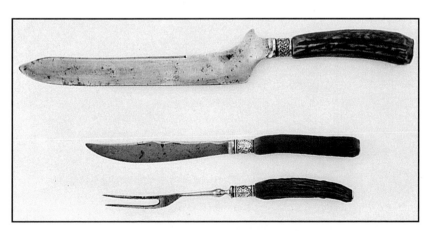

Carving set, 3-piece, stag handles, logo on sterling silver ferrules, nickel caps, $50.00 – 65.00.

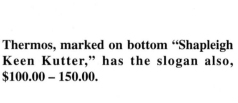

Carving knife with 9" blade, $20.00 – 30.00; steak or chop carver set, 2-piece, stag handles, sterling ferrules with logo on them, $65.00 – 85.00.

Thermos, marked on bottom "Shapleigh Keen Kutter," has the slogan also, $100.00 – 150.00.

Water jug, Shapleigh, insulated, faucet spigot type, $75.00 – 100.00.

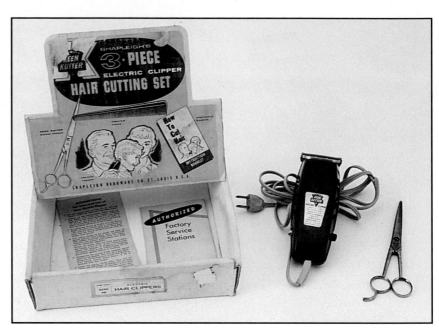

Electric hair cutting set in display box, double sided top display, has papers, missing comb, $75.00 – 100.00 set.

Sewing machine needles, tin case, 11½" long x 7½" wide, 2½" high with hinged cover, 132-tube assortment, $275.00 – 325.00.

Sewing machine, Volo treadle machine marked "E. C. Simmons" on the pedal. The keyholes in the drawers have the brass Keen Kutter logo for keyhole covers. It has a brass key as well as a small screwdriver marked Keen Kutter, $350.00 – 400.00.

LEVELS

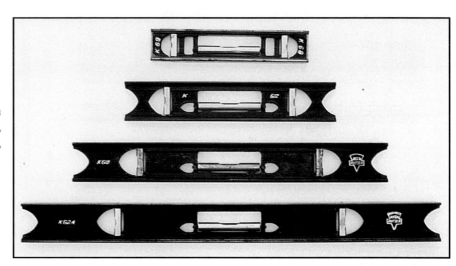

Levels, cast iron, K69, 9", $290.00 auction price; K612, 12", $175.00 – 225.00; K618, 18" adjustable, $150.00 – 200.00; K624, 24", $175.00 – 225.00.

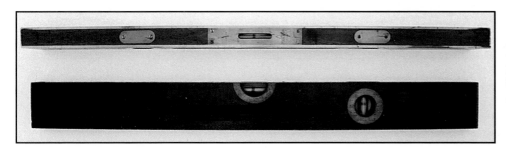

Levels, adjustable, brass tip, top plate, brass bound, 30", KK40, $150.00 – 225.00; KK45 has double duplex plates, $150.00 – 225.00.

Levels, both KK50, adjustable, brass tip, top plate, brass bound, 26", $150.00 – 225.00; 30", $150.00 – 225.00.

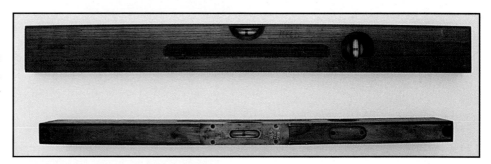

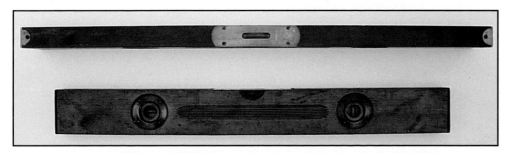

Levels, both KK30, adjustable, brass tip, top plate, double duplex plates. Pat. 12-20-04 on face plate. 30", $75.00 – 100.00; 26", $75.00 – 100.00.

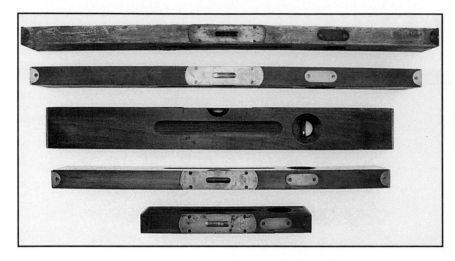

Levels, adjustable, cast-brass tips and top plate, 30", KK3, $45.00 – 65.00; 28", KK3, $45.00 – 65.00; 26", KK3, $45.00 – 65.00; 24", KK3, $45.00 – 65.00; 12", KS3, $75.00 – 100.00.

Levels, both KK2, adjustable, brass top plate, 30" has square name plate, $30.00 – 35.00; 28", $30.00 – 35.00.

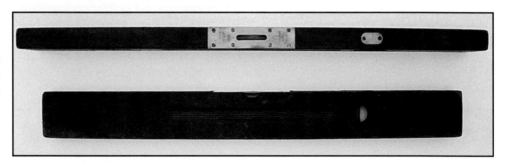

Levels, all KK13, non-adjustable, brass top plate, 18", $40.00 – 65.00; 16", $40.00 – 65.00; 12", $50.00 – 75.00.

Levels, all KK104, non-adjustable, brass top plate, 18", $40.00 – 65.00; 14", $40.00 – 65.00; 12", $40.00 – 65.00.

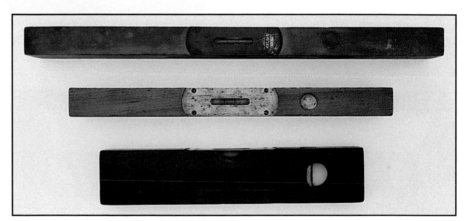

Levels, all KKO, non-adjustable, brass top. 30", $30.00 – 35.00; 28", $30.00 – 35.00; 26", $30.00 – 35.00; 24", $30.00 – 35.00.

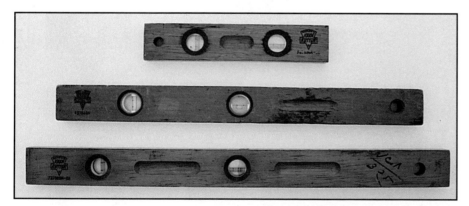

Masonry level KK25, adjustable, brass button with logo, $65.00 – 95.00.

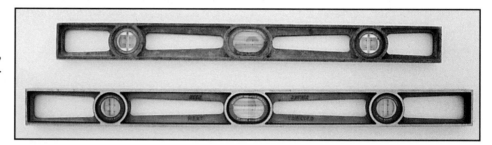

Levels, Shapleigh cast aluminum, 24", $45.00 – 65.00; 28", $45.00 – 65.00. Auction price (mint), $105.00.

Levels, Shapleigh, non-adjustable, F3-753GK 12", $50.00 – 75.00; F3-754GK 24", $45.00 – 65.00; F3-755GK 28", $45.00 – 65.00.

Pocket or torpedo levels, F3764GK wooden 9", $50.00 – 75.00; cast aluminum, 8¾", $50.00 – 75.00.

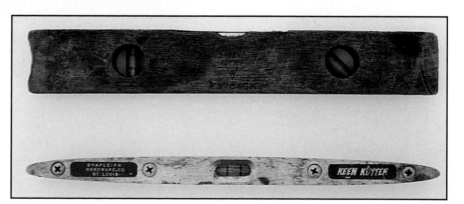

Keen Kutter railroad padlocks, front and back views, logo-shaped, E. C. Simmons on one side of shackle, St. Louis U.S.A. on other. Santa Fe Signal with dust cover, auction price, $475.00; Santa Fe General, auction price, $425.00.

Padlock display holder, wooden, 27" tall x 6¾" wide. Holds 12 locks on the front and 12 on the back. Both sides are the same design. $750.00 – 1,000.00.

Padlocks, front and back views, regular size Keen Kutter logo-shaped padlock and small padlock. Regular size, $200.00; small size, $600.00.

Padlocks, front and back views of four different Keen Kutter logo-shaped locks with "E. C. Simmons" written on one side of the shackle and "St. Louis U.S.A." written on the other, $100.00 – 125.00 each; with original key, $150.00 – 175.00 each.

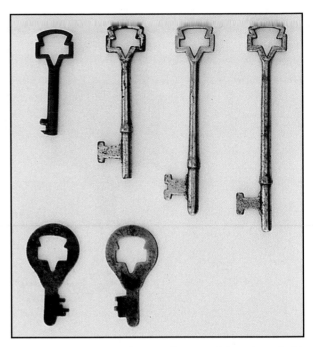

Brass skeleton key for sewing machine (top left), $35.00 – 50.00; skeleton keys, emblem-shaped, $8.00 – 15.00 each; padlock keys, emblem-shaped, one has key cut flat and other bent, $15.00 – 25.00 each.

Trunk lock with key, $175.00 – 225.00.

Padlocks, front and back views of four different Keen Kutter logo-shaped locks with "E. C. Simmons" written on one side of the shackle and "St. Louis U.S.A." written on the other side, $100.00 – 125.00 each; with original key, $150.00 – 175.00 each.

Padlocks, not Keen Kutter. Front and back views of these three railroad locks with Keen Kutter logo appearance. The locks are often mistaken for Keen Kutter ones, but there is no association with the company other than appearance.

PAPER GOODS

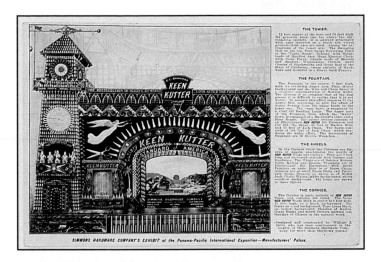

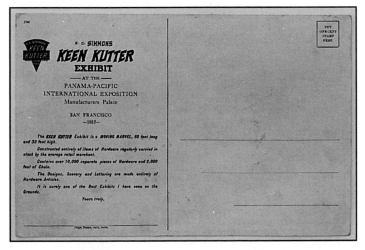

Postcard, 1915, showing both back and front. Simmons Hardware Company's exhibit at the Panama-Pacific International Exposition, San Francisco. The exhibit was 60' long, 33' high, containing over 10,000 pieces of hardware and 2,000 feet of chain, $300.00 – 350.00.

Postcards. Top: 1909, hatchet with dog, $175.00 – 225.00; Middle: 1909, like velvet, lawn mower, $125.00 – 200.00; Bottom: 1944, old truck (possible reproduction), $25.00.

Seal or collector's stamp for prize redemption at the St. Louis World's Fair. Reads: John Shaw & Sons Wolverhampton Ltd. Trade Mark JS&S Made in U.S.A. Simmons Hardware Co'Y Sole Distributors of the "Keen Kutter" "True Blue" "Oak Leaf" "Black Jack" & "Chip-A-Way" brands. $100.00.

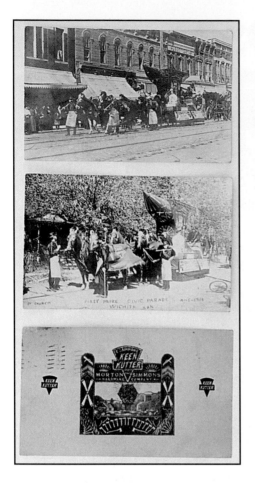

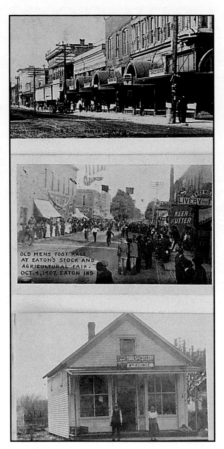

Left:
Postcards, Wichita, Kansas. Top: 1908 civic parade, 1st prize float, "Morton-Simmons" on large anvil, $200.00 – 250.00; Center: Same, closer view showing even horses decorated, $200.00 – 250.00. Bottom: 1911 Morton Simmons Hardware exhibit at the Wichita Exposition titled "It's A Corker", $75.00 – 125.00.

Right:
Postcards. Top: Street scene 1908 Poplar Bluff, Mo., Keen Kutter sign hangs on store front, $75.00 – 125.00. Center: 1907 "Old Men's Foot Race" at Agricultural Fair, Eaton, Ind., emblem on store front to right, $75.00 – 125.00. Bottom: Man and woman outside Wm. Klinge Hardware Store, no date, $75.00 – 125.00.

Trade cards, various types where hardware store would send regarding an order, or a salesman would send to say what date to expect him, $35.00 – 65.00 each.

Trade cards with old shield emblem. Left: 1904, salesman would mail out telling what date to expect him, $125.00 – 150.00. Right: The back contains a "Sales Pitch" encouraging customers to buy Keen Kutter, $125.00 – 150.00.

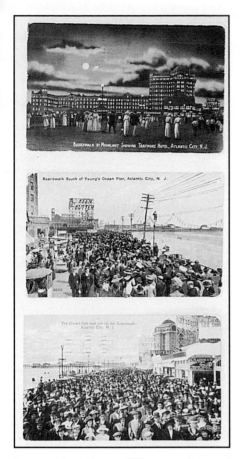

Postcards. Three different views of the Boardwalk, Atlantic City, New Jersey. Top: 1913 night scene, $50.00 – 75.00. Center: 1911 Keen Kutter very visible, $30.00 – 60.00. Bottom: 1914 Keen Kutter less visible, $30.00 – 60.00.

Mail flyer, sale bill fall circular No. 2, year 1900, containing double-sided advertisement, 23" x 8¼", $75.00 – 100.00.

Mail flyer, sale bill containing 8 pages, 12½" x 8¼", Winchester-Simmons Co., $150.00 – 200.00.

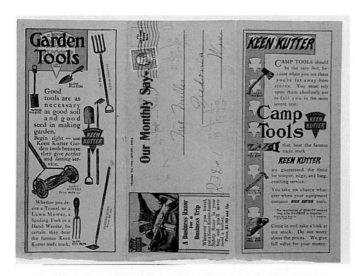

Advertising circular, 9" x 12", ads on both sides, folds up to 9" x 4" for mailing, $75.00 – 100.00.

Simmons Service War Bulletin, dated August 1918, series of approximately twelve pages, each filled with valuable war information, $75.00 – 100.00 each.

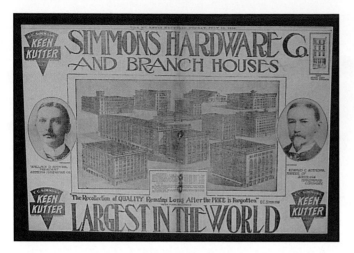

Newspaper page, 32½" x 22", from *St. Louis Republic* dated July 12, 1908, showing Simmons' warehouses. $250.00 – 300.00.

Shapleigh stand-up advertisements, size 7¾" x 5½", National Series 2328, Two Great Rivers, the Missouri and Mississippi; National Series 2336, Founders Month, $125.00 – 175.00 each.

Invoices, 1890 and early 1900s, showing buildings, $15.00 – 20.00 each.

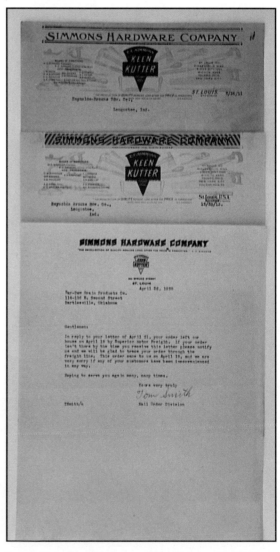

Letterheads, Simmons Hardware Company, $10.00 – 15.00 each.

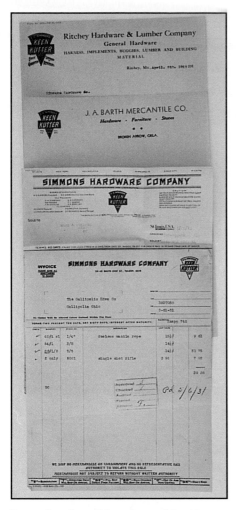

Letterhead and invoices of hardware stores, $7.00 – 15.00 each.

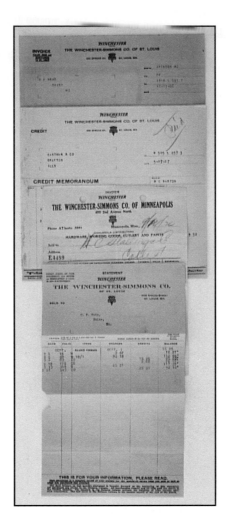

Winchester-Simmons Company 1926 and 1927 invoices, credit memo and statement, $7.00 – 15.00 each.

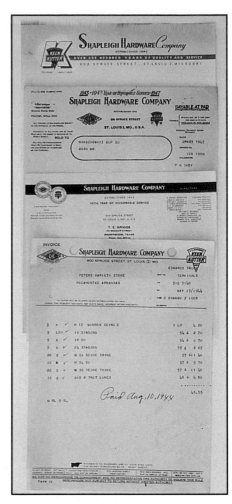

Letterhead and invoice, Shapleigh Hardware Company, $7.00 – 15.00 each.

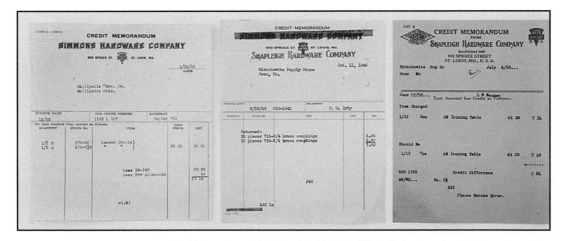

Credit memorandums, $7.00 – 15.00 each.

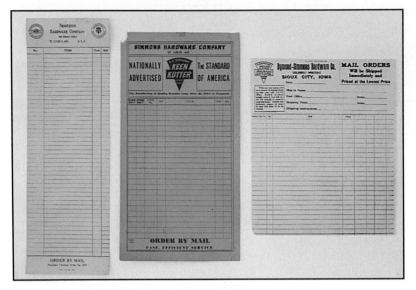

Order-by-mail forms, $7.00 – 15.00 each.

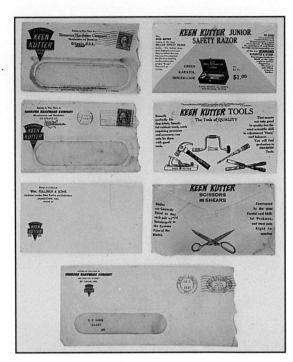

Envelopes, colorful and artistic fronts and backs, $35.00 – 40.00 each.

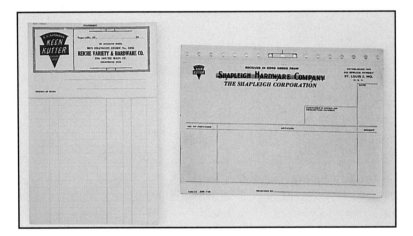

Statement, 5½" x 8½", $15.00 – 20.00; received goods order form, carbonized, 8½" x 6¼", $10.00 – 15.00.

Envelopes, Winchester-Simmons Company. Inside the envelope are invoices dated 1926 and 1927, $35.00 – 40.00 with invoice.

Envelopes, various styles and sizes, $10.00 – 20.00 each.

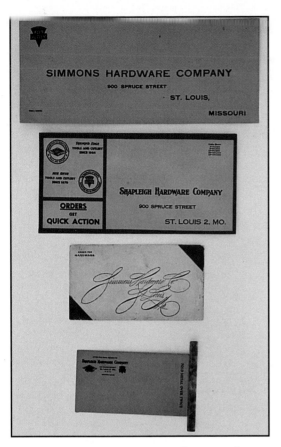

Envelopes. Top two are order envelopes, manila, $15.00 – 25.00 each; envelope pre-addressed with fancy long hand, $20.00 – 30.00; parts envelope, manila, has metal type fold-over seal, $15.00 – 20.00.

Receipt pad, carbonized, 6" x 3½", $25.00 – 35.00.

Tie-on price tags. Large 3", emblem-shaped, $40.00 – 60.00; small 1" emblem-shaped, $25.00 – 35.00; oval, $4.00 – 6.00; round, $3.00 – 5.00; square, $2.00 – 3.00.

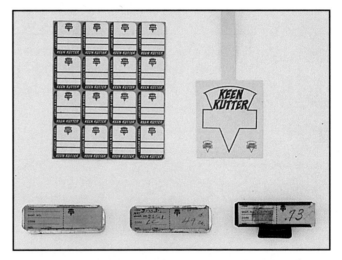

Pricing tags and labels. Sheet of self-adhesive stickers, $10.00 – 15.00; cardboard handled price tag, $20.00 – 25.00; bin labels, $10.00 – 15.00 each.

Box of Hi-Low bin tickets, $75.00 – 100.00; roll of shipping tape, $75.00 – 80.00.

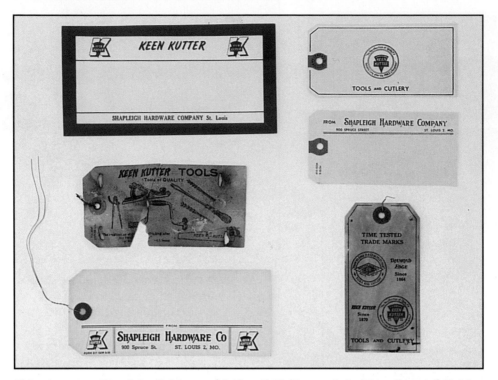

Shipping tags. Top left: Stick-on, $3.00 – 5.00. Lower left: Two tie-on, $10.00 – 15.00 each. Top right: Front and back, $5.00 – 7.00. Lower right: Tie-on DE & KK, $12.00 – 18.00.

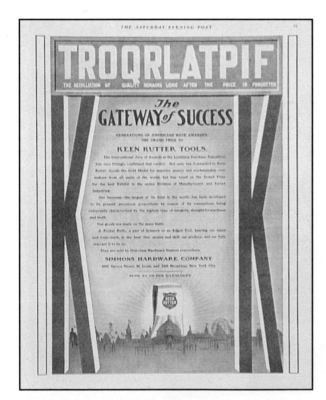

1904 *Saturday Evening Post* advertisement, $35.00 – 40.00.

1907 *Saturday Evening Post* advertisement, $25.00 – 30.00.

Color magazine ad, 8¼" x 11½", $25.00 – 35.00.

Top: Magazine advertisement in color, 6½" x 9", "The Dog Doesn't Mind, He Knows It Won't Hurt – It's a Keen Kutter," back side is a Kellogg's Corn Flakes ad dated 1910, $150.00 – 225.00. Bottom: Magazine ad in black and white, 6½" x 9", $125.00 – 150.00.

Magazine advertisements, sizes 6¾" x 10", $10.00 – 15.00 each.

PLANES

Wooden planes with saw tooth logo. Left to right: 26", $75.00 – 100.00; 20", $65.00 – 85.00; 15", $65.00 – 85.00; 10", $75.00 – 95.00. This was probably one of their first markings, the half-moon shape with saw tooth design. It appears on the front wood base as well as the blade.

Fore planes, E. C. Simmons, all wooden. Left to right: 30", $100.00 – 175.00; 26", $75.00 – 100.00; 24", $75.00 – 100.00; 15", $75.00 – 100.00; 15", $75.00 – 125.00, back slants, cut lower. All marked in front of knob and on blade.

Coffin plane, 8", shaped like a coffin. Most markings are on the front but occasionally they are on the side as shown here. $50.00 – 75.00.

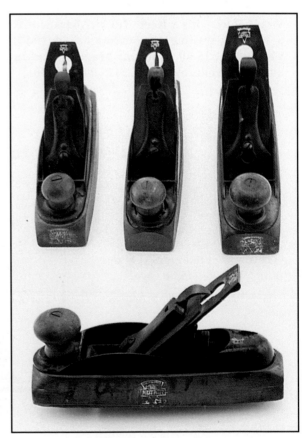

Wood bottom smooth adjustable planes: K22, 8" with 1¾" blade, $45.00 – 75.00; K23, 9" with 1¾" blade, $45.00 – 75.00; K24, 9" with 2" blade, $45.00 – 75.00. Front one: K23 marked on side instead of front, $45.00 – 75.00.

Wood bottom planes. Left to right: K31, 24", $65.00 – 85.00; K28, 18" fore style, $50.00 – 75.00; K27, $50.00 – 75.00; K26, 15" jack style, $50.00 – 75.00.

K35, smooth wood bottom handled plane with saw tooth logo, $75.00 – 100.00; K35 with regular logo, $65.00 – 85.00.

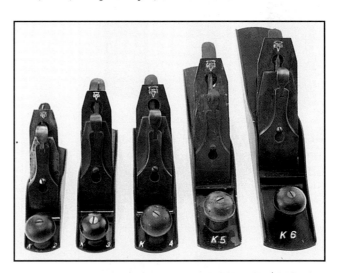

Iron planes with smooth bottoms: K2, 7", $550.00 – 750.00; K3, 8", $75.00 – 125.00; K4, 9", $50.00 – 75.00; K5, 14" jack style, $50.00 – 75.00; K6, 18" fore style, $75.00 – 100.00.

K2 iron plane with smooth bottom, $550.00 – 750.00; K2 iron plane with corrugated bottom, $750.00 – 1,000.00.

Iron planes with corrugated bottoms: K2, 7", $750.00 – 1,000.00; K3, 8", $150.00 – 200.00; K4, 9", $50.00 – 75.00; K4½, 10", $75.00 – 125.00; K5 turned to show corrugated bottom, $50.00 – 75.00; K5½, 15" jack plane, $75.00 – 100.00; K6, 18" fore plane, $75.00 – 100.00.

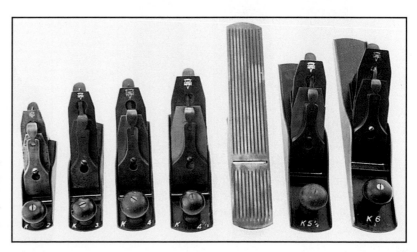

Iron planes: K8 jointer, smooth bottom, $100.00 – 150.00; KK7 jointer, corrugated bottom, $75.00 – 125.00; K7 jointer, corrugated bottom, $75.00 – 125.00.

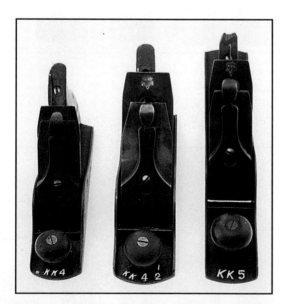

Iron planes: KK4 corrugated, $65.00 – 85.00; KK4½, 10", 2⅜" cutter, smooth bottom, $100.00 – 125.00; KK5 corrugated, $65.00 – 85.00.

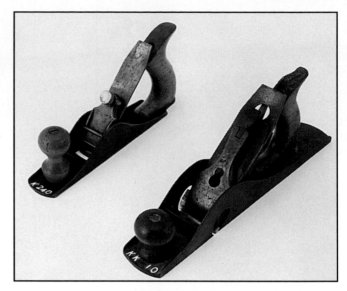

K240 scrub plane, $125.00 – 175.00; KK10 carriage maker's rabbet plane, $200.00 – 250.00.

Plane, KK10½, smooth bottom with adjustable throat, blade marked "E. C. Simmons," rare, $600.00 – 800.00.

Iron planes, smooth bottom, with logos only on lever caps: 8", $65.00 – 85.00; 9", $50.00 – 75.00; 14", $50.00 – 75.00.

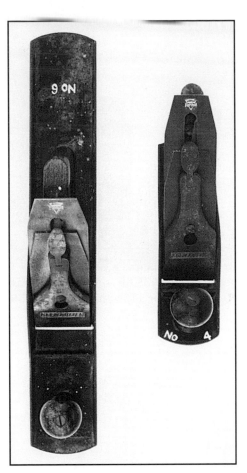

KK No. 5 plane, $125.00 – 175.00.

No. 4 iron plane, $60.00 – 80.00; No. 6 iron plane, $70.00 – 90.00. Both have "Keen Kutter" written on lever cap.

KKM4 iron smooth plane in original box. Complete with box, $150.00 – 225.00; KKM4, no box, $50.00 – 75.00.

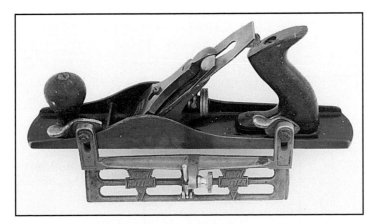

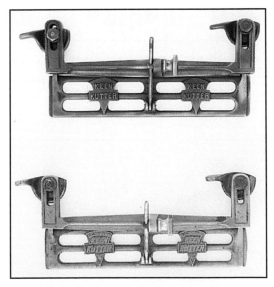

K5 jack plane with fence, smooth bottom with jointer or plane gauge attachment, adjustable angels between 30° and 90°. Plane value, $50.00 – 75.00; attachment value, $100.00 – 135.00.

Fences or jointer plane gauges with adjustable angles between 30° and 90°, overall length 9". Keen Kutter only logo, $90.00 – 120.00; E. C. Simmons logo, $100.00 – 135.00.

Replacement handle for a plane, $30.00.

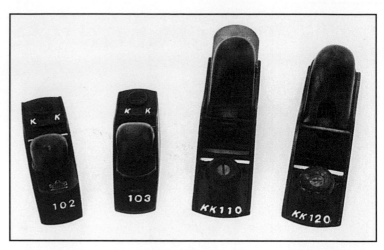

Iron block planes, KK102, $35.00 – 50.00; KK103 with lever adjustment, $35.00 – 50.00; KK110, $35.00 – 50.00; KK120, 7½" with lever adjustment, $35.00 – 50.00.

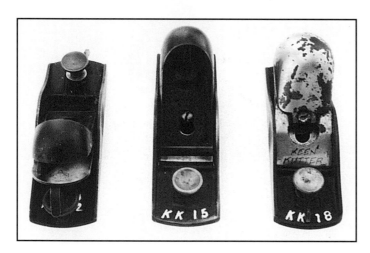

Iron block planes, KK9½ adjustable 6", $50.00 – 75.00; KK15 7", $35.00 – 50.00; KK18 knuckle joint adjustable, $50.00 – 75.00.

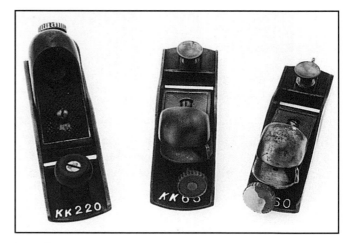

Iron block planes, lateral adjustment done by moving block to which back knob is attached. KK220, $200.00 – 275.00; KK65, $200.00 – 275.00; KK60 low angle 6" with marking on blade, $200.00 – 275.00.

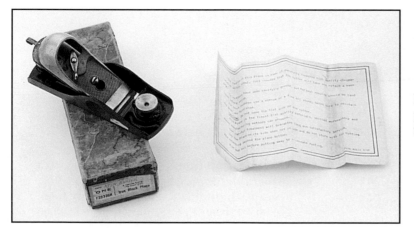

Iron block plane, K9½, 6" in original box with papers, $150.00 – 200.00; without box or papers, $35.00 – 55.00.

Iron block planes: KK9¾, 6" with screw lever and throat adjustment, rosewood handle, cutter 1¾", $375.00 – 450.00; KK140, 7" rabbet and block, 1¾" cutter, $450.00 – 550.00.

Iron block planes: K220, 7½" adjustable, old style cap, $35.00 – 50.00; K130, 8" non-adjustable double ender, reversible (one for block and one for bullnose, cutter 1⅝"), $75.00 – 100.00; K120, 7½" with lever adjustment, 1⅝" cutter, $35.00 – 50.00; K110, 7½" non-adjustable 1⅝" cutter, $35.00 – 50.00; K110, unmarked, $30.00 – 35.00; K102, 5½" non adjustable, 1¼" cutter, $35.00 – 50.00; K140, adjustable with removable side fence, $175.00 – 225.00.

K64 Adjustable iron plane, combination, beading, rabbet and slitting combined, nickel plated cast iron frame, rosewood handles, 21 highest grade crucible steel cutters in a brown canvas roll complete with a K50/2 Keen Kutter screwdriver, $800.00; with original box, auction price, $1,750.00.

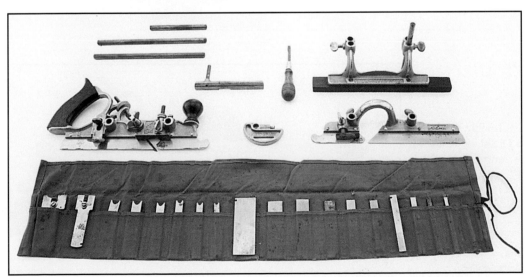

Router plane, K171, patented date 10-29-01, length 7½", $150.00 – 200.00.

Circular planes, will cut concave or convex: K200, $500.00 – 700.00; KK115, $350.00 – 550.00.

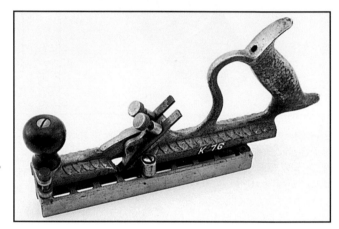

K76 tongue and groove, swing fence plane, $175.00 – 250.00.

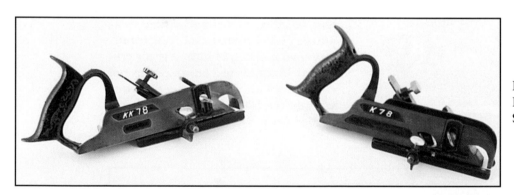

Rabbet and filletster planes, KK78, $175.00 – 250.00; K78, $175.00 – 250.00.

Rabbet planes, KK190, 8" with 1½" cutter, $175.00 – 250.00; K191, 8" with 1½" cutter, $175.00 – 250.00; K192, 8" with 1" cutter, $175.00 – 250.00.

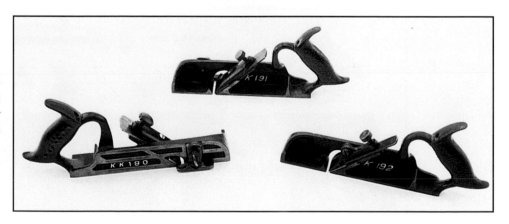

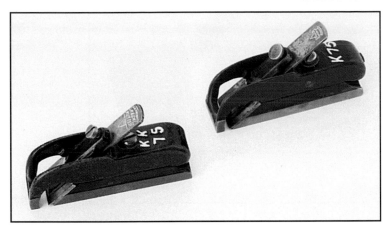

Bullnose rabbet plane, KK75 and K75, non adjustable, 4", $150.00 – 175.00 each.

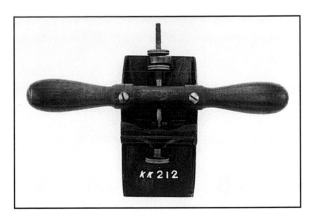

KK212 scraper and chamfer plane, $200.00 – 275.00.

Cabinet scraper planes, KK80, $100.00 – 125.00; KK79 chrome, $50.00 – 60.00; KK79, $50.00 – 60.00; K79, $50.00 – 60.00.

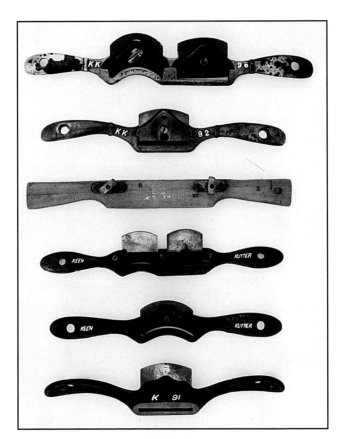

Spoke shaves: KK96 CI frame, straight and concave cutters, $100.00 – 125.00; KK92 CI frame, straight cutter, $55.00 – 75.00; KK90 wooden beechwood, straight cutter, $75.00 – 100.00; K97 CI frame, straight and concave cutters, $100.00 – 125.00; K95 CI frame, concave cutter, $55.00 – 75.00; K91 CI frame, straight cutter, $55.00 – 75.00.

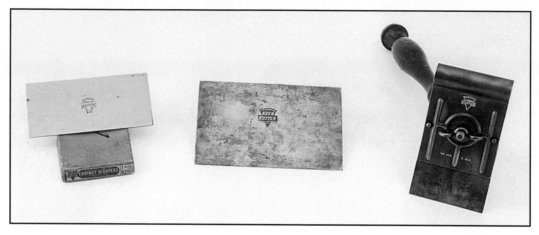

Left to right: K255 flat steel cabinet scraper, 2½" x 5", and a box that one dozen came in, $100.00 – 150.00; cabinet scraper, 4" x 6", $35.00 – 45.00; floor and cabinet scraper with handle, $35.00 – 45.00.

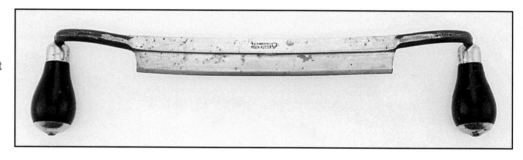

Draw knife, KLP 8", with offset handles, $100.00 – 125.00.

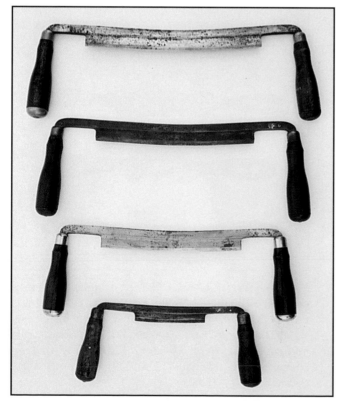

Draw knives, all with logo on blade and on top toward right handle: K10, 10" blade, $35.00 – 55.00; K9, 9" blade, $35.00 – 55.00; K8, 8" blade, $35.00 – 55.00; K4, 4" blade, $150.00 – 175.00.

PLIERS

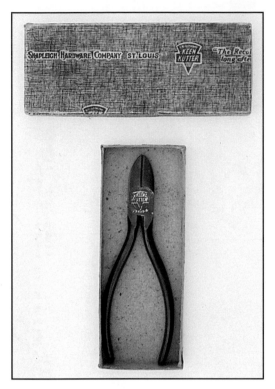

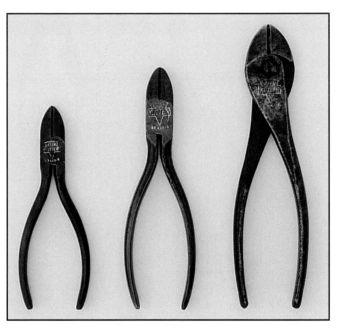

Diagonal cutting pliers, K45-5", $30.00 – 40.00; K45-6", $30.00 – 40.00; K47-7", $30.00 – 40.00.

K45-5 diagonal cutting pliers in original box, $100.00 – 150.00; pliers alone, $30.00 – 40.00.

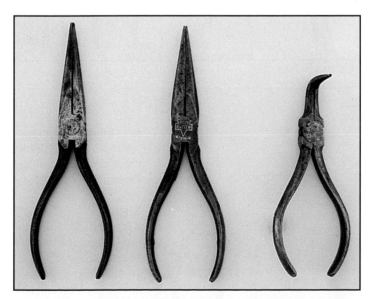

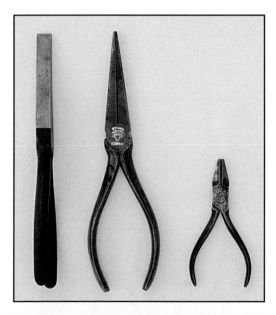

Left: K66-6 round nose pliers, $30.00 – 40.00. Center: K76-6 Side cutting pliers with extra long nose, $30.00 – 40.00. Right: milliner's or radio pliers, $75.00 – 100.00.

Flat nose pliers, left: side view K86-6, ⅜" wide, flat nose pliers, $40.00 – 45.00. Center: ¼" wide, $40.00 – 45.00. Right: ³⁄₁₆" wide x 3¼" long, $75.00 – 100.00.

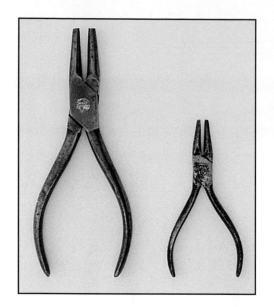

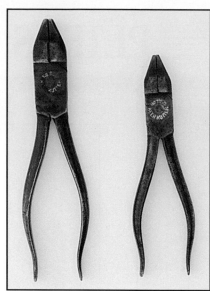

Left:
Round nose pliers. Left: 5¼", $30.00 – 40.00. Right: 3½", $75.00 – 100.00.

Right:
Raised side cutter pliers. Left: No. 950, 7½", $25.00 – 35.00. Right: No. 950, 6", $25.00 – 35.00.

Right:
Heavy pattern pliers with raised side cutter. Left: 8½", $30.00 – 40.00. Center: 7½", $30.00 – 40.00. Right: 6", $30.00 – 40.00.

Left:
Side cutting pliers, heavy duty. Left: regular logo, $30.00 – 40.00. Right: K85-8, regular logo with other side marked St.L-SFR.R (railroad) $100.00 – 125.00.

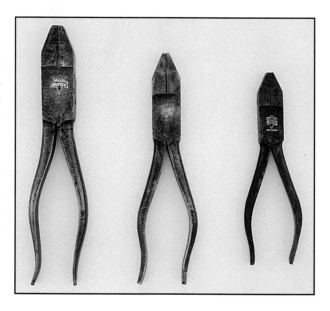

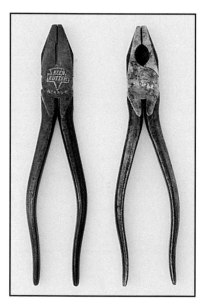

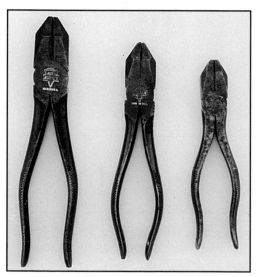

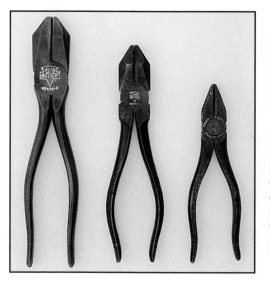

Left:
Klein pattern lineman pliers. Left: 8½", $30.00 – 40.00. Center: 7½", $30.00 – 40.00. Right: 6½", $30.00 – 40.00.

Right:
Klein pattern lineman pliers. Left: No. K96-8, $30.00 – 40.00. Center: 7¼", $30.00 – 40.00. Right: 6" light flat nose side cutters that have "Keen Kutter" written out plus the logo, $30.00 – 40.00.

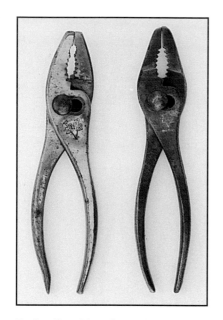

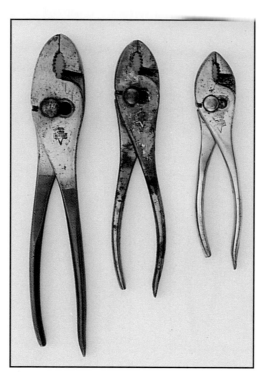

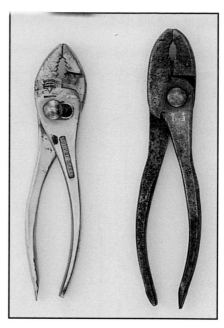

Left: Combination pliers, 6½", thin narrow 30° bent nose slip joint with screwdriver handle, $35.00 – 45.00. Right: Combination pliers, 6½" straight nose, $30.00 – 35.00.

Combination pliers, gas and flat nose pliers wire cutter, pipe wrench and screwdriver wire cutter on side. Each has screwdriver on end of handle. Sizes 7", 8", and 10", $20.00 – 30.00 each.

Left: Slip-joint pliers with screwdriver end, $20.00 – 30.00. Right: Slip-joint pliers with wire cutters on bottom, one of the first, very unusual, $25.00 – 35.00.

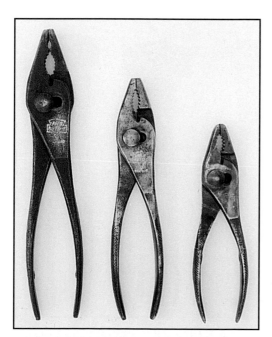

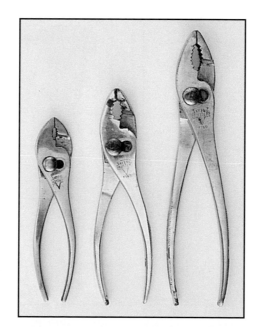

K51, 10", 8", 6" combination pliers with cutters in middle, $25.00 – 30.00 each.

Slip joint pliers. Left to right: 5½", $30.00 – 45.00; K160, $20.00 – 30.00; K180, $20.00 – 30.00.

Pistol grip pliers, KK7 with wording: Pat. Applied For Shapleigh Hardware Co. St. Louis, $125.00 – 175.00.

Gas pipe and battery pliers. 10",
$25.00 – 35.00; 8", $25.00 – 35.00; 6",
$25.00 – 35.00.

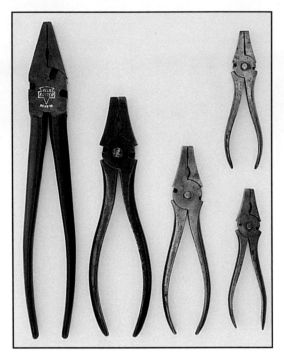

Left to right: Pliers and wire cutter combined. KB10, 10½" long, $30.00 – 45.00; 8"
with name written on handle with patent date
2/5/01, $30.00 – 45.00; 6¼" long, $30.00 –
45.00; 4¾" closed type with patent date,
$45.00 – 65.00; 4¾" open type with patent
date, $45.00 – 65.00.

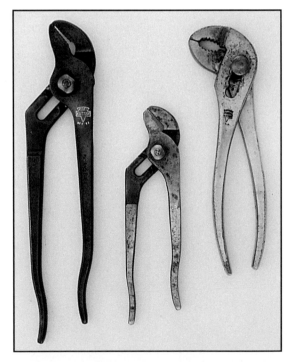

Left: Pump pliers K57, 9½", $85.00 – 115.00.
Center: Pump pliers K507, 6½", $85.00 –
115.00. Right: Combination plier and pipe
wrench K750, 75° angle head, $85.00 – 115.00.

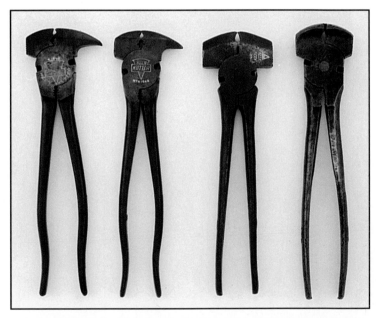

Staple pullers. Left two are K1946 with different markings,
fencing pliers or staple pullers, 10¼" long with 2⅝" heads,
$35.00 – 40.00 each; 10¼" combination staple puller, driver,
wire cutter, splicer, and bolt grip, $35.00 – 40.00; 10¼" narrow
nose with sharp edge, $35.00 – 40.00.

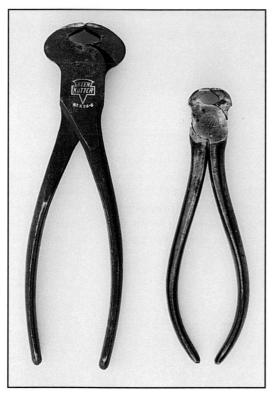

Cutting nippers. Left: K26-6, $30.00 – 45.00.
Right: 5", $30.00 – 45.00.

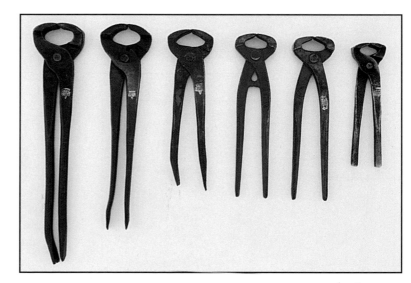

Cardboard boxes for two different sizes of carpenter pincers,
$20.00 – 30.00 each.

Carpenter pincers: 12" with claw and screwdriver handle, $15.00 –
20.00; 10" with claw and screwdriver handle, $15.00 – 20.00; 8"
with claw and screwdriver handle, $20.00 – 25.00; 8", no claw or
screwdriver, $20.00 – 25.00; 8", no claw or screwdriver, $20.00 –
25.00; 6", no claw or screwdriver, $25.00 – 30.00.

Cutting nippers, sizes 6" and 8", jaws are reversible and
interchangeable with two cutting edges held by two screws,
logo on one cutter and handle, $30.00 – 45.00 each.

POCKET KNIVES

Silent salesman electric pocket knife display. The wooden case has a slant design and measures 19½" wide x 9" deep x 13" high. Attached to top of the case is a 18" x 3¼" two-bladed knife. When turned on, the blades continuously move up and down. Behind the front glass 15 knives can be displayed. There is a storage area in back for extra stock. Without knives, $6,500.00 – 7,000.00.

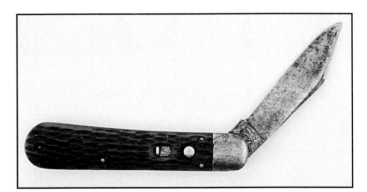

Switch blade with stag handle, US patents of Dec. 21, 1909 and Sept. 13, 1910, $400.00 – 500.00.

Pocket knives revolving display case, four sides, 11" square x 18½" tall. Top lifts off to change knives, storage area in center. Without knives, $250.00 – 350.00.

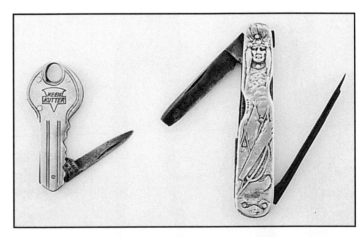

Key chain knife, $100.00 – 125.00; knife, Indian design No. K4840SS, sterling silver handle, broken blade. As is, $40.00 – 50.00; good condition, $200.00 – 225.00.

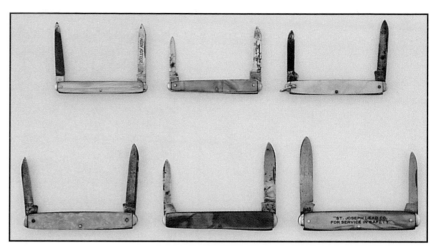

Two-bladed knives with celluloid handles. Top row: white pearl handle, No.27122 and K18 vest knife, $40.00 – 100.00 depending on condition. Bottom row: K863C, no number, green handle; No. 840 St. Joe Lead Co. For Service in Safety, $40.00 – 100.00 depending on condition.

Iron handled, black enameled knives. K1787 single blade embossed, $100.00 – 150.00; #2787 double blade embossed, $100.00 – 150.00; K2787 double blade, not embossed, marked on blade, $50.00 – 100.00.

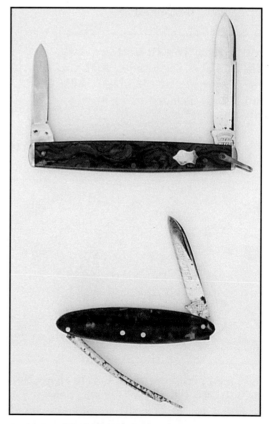

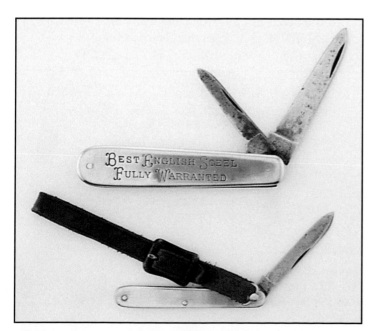

Best English steel knife No. 2909 with German silver handle, fully warranted, $50.00 – 100.00; pocket fob knife, knob turns to open knife, nickel silver handle, $75.00 – 100.00.

Top: No. 0214TK pocket vest knife, excellent condition, marked on blade, $100.00 – 150.00; K0650C with nail file, $100.00 – 150.00.

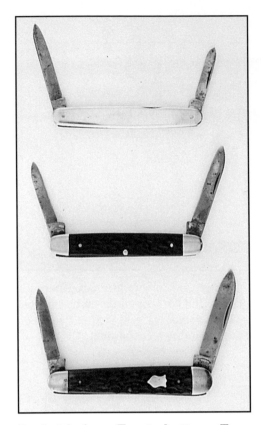

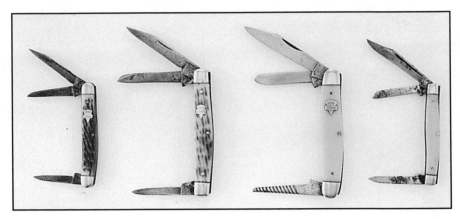

Pocket knives, three-bladed stag handle. Left to right: No. 886 stag handle, No. 769 celluloid handle, No. 793 celluloid handle, $40.00 – 100.00 each depending on condition.

Pocket knives. Top to bottom: Two-bladed, nickel silver handle, K21 stag handle pen knife, K0198 stag handle, $45.00 – 100.00 each depending on condition.

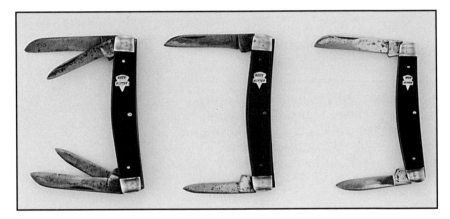

Congress knives. Left to right: #773 four-bladed, #767 two-bladed, #790 two-bladed, $40.00 – 100.00 each depending on condition.

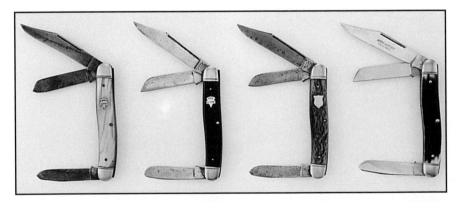

Three-bladed premium stock. Left to right: No. 861 white nupearl celluloid handle, $50.00 – 100.00; No. 772 stag handle, $50.00 – 100.00; K12 stag handle, $50.00 – 100.00; No. 881 stag handle, handmade, one of the last Keen Kutter knives made by Shapleigh, mint condition, $150.00 – 175.00.

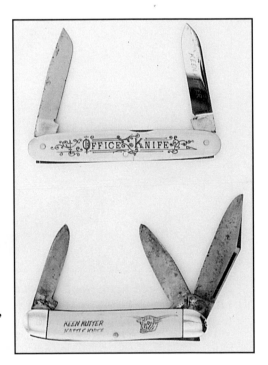

K02220 office knife, white celluloid handle with etching, mint, $200.00; K394 kattle knife, $125.00 – 175.00.

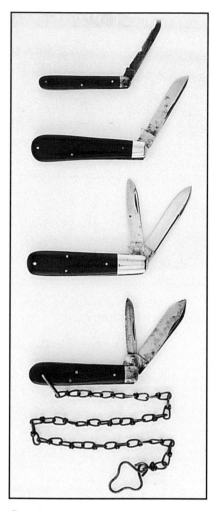

Barlow pattern knives. Top left: K254 brown bone handle, 3¼'', $40.00 – 100.00 depending on condition. Top right: K2281¾ brown handle, 3⅜'', $40.00 – 100.00 depending on condition. Bottom left: No. 882 black bone handle, $40.00 – 100.00 depending on condition. Bottom right: K2884¾ white celluloid handle, 3¼'', $40.00 – 100.00 depending on condition.

Cocobolo handled knives. Top to bottom: 2½'' single blade, $40.00 – 100.00; 3'' single blade, $40.00 – 100.00; 3¼'' two-bladed, $40.00 – 100.00; 3⅜'' two-bladed, with chain, $80.00 – 95.00.

Pruning knives with cocobolo handles. Left to right: KS105, extra heavy, 4⅜'', $45.00 – 65.00; KS106, 4'', $45.00 – 65.00; 3½'' length, mint, $75.00 – 100.00.

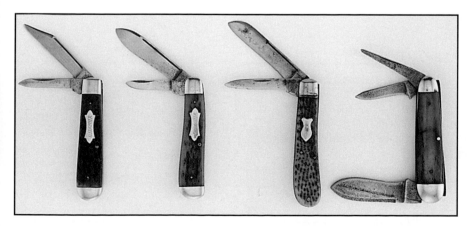

Pocket knives. Left to right: K53¾ two-bladed; K98C two-bladed; no number, two-bladed; no number, very thick three-bladed, $40.00 – 100.00 each depending on condition.

Left to right: No. 658 outdoor knife with stag handle, $90.00 – 140.00; K100 large saber clip blade, red celluloid handle, $75.00 – 100.00; No. 843 scout knife, $100.00 – 125.00.

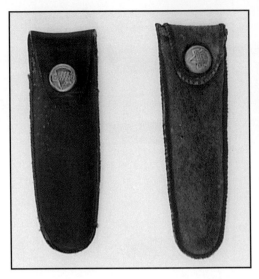

Knife purses with brass buttons embossed with logo, $40.00 – 60.00 each.

Cardboard pocket knife boxes, various sizes, $20.00 – 35.00 each.

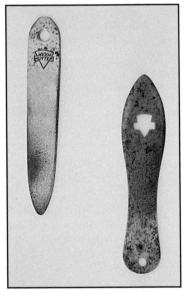

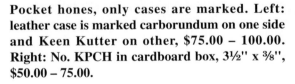

Tissue paper that pocket knives were wrapped in when shipped, $20.00 – 25.00.

Knife picks, used to open pocket knives. Left: $200.00 – 250.00. Right: $175.00 – 225.00.

Pocket hones, only cases are marked. Left: leather case is marked carborundum on one side and Keen Kutter on other, $75.00 – 100.00. Right: No. KPCH in cardboard box, 3½'' x ⅜'', $50.00 – 75.00.

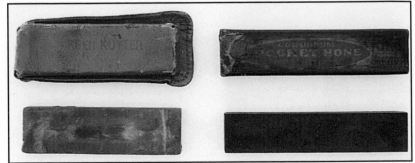

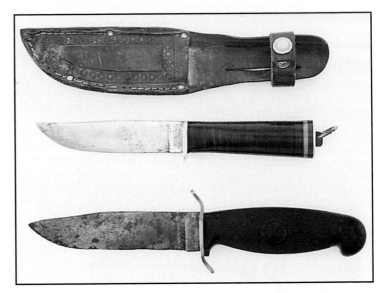

Hunting knives, Simmons with marked sheaths. Top: 5" blade marked "Simmons Hardware Co. St. Louis, USA," stag handle, $300.00 – 375.00. Bottom: 4" marked blade, leather handle, $150.00 – 200.00.

KBK94 hunting knife, leather handle with red and white fibre end laminations and the original nickel silver guard and end plate with ring for strap. Has sheath, overall 7¾", $150.00 – 200.00; KBK25 hunting knife, checkered black hard rubber handle with heavy brass double guard, overall 9½", $50.00 – 100.00. Both of these are in the 1939 catalog.

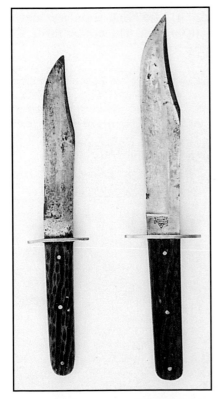

E. C. Simmons hunting knives with swaged blades and stag handles. Left: No. 1050, 5" blade, $100.00 – 150.00. Right: 6" blade with "Keen Kutter" written on blade and logo, $150.00 – 200.00.

Hunting knives, Shapleigh with unmarked sheaths. Top: 4½" blade with logo and leather handle, $125.00 – 175.00. Bottom: 4" blade with logo and leather handle, $125.00 – 175.00.

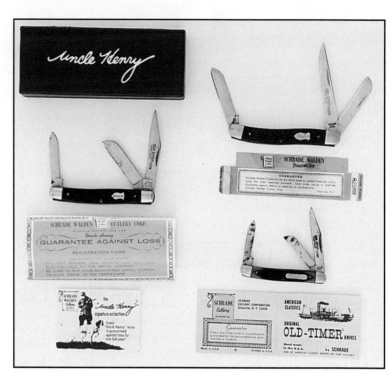

Schrade-Walden Cutlery knives with "Keen Kutter" written on blades. Old Timer K1050T, K825RB stainless, and an Uncle Henry K874, $25.00 – 40.00 each. These were made after Shapleigh went out of business.

Spirit of St. Louis #K74, Limited Edition, 12,000 were made in the USA, this one is serial #4352, $65.00 – 90.00.

Pocket knives made since 1991, some still current from Frost Cutlery, Chattanooga, TN. Retail, $25.00 – 60.00 each. Wholesale, $12.00 – 30.00 each.

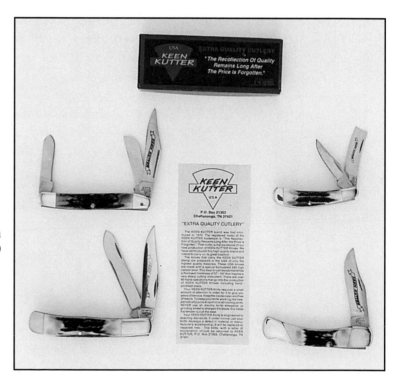

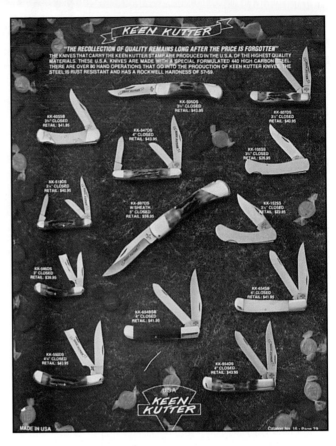

Page from *Frost Cutlery* magazine, Chattanooga, TN, showing different styles of Keen Kutter pocket knives manufactured beginning in 1991. There are a few currently available.

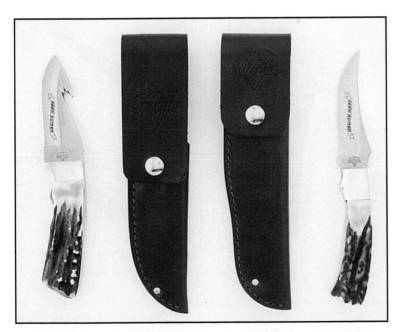

Hunting knives with sheaths made since 1991, some still current, from Frost Cutlery, Chattanooga, TN. Retail, $75.00 each. Wholesale, $35.00 each.

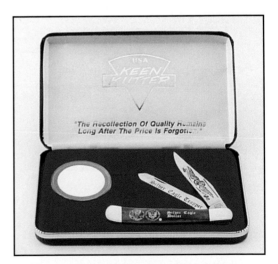

Frost Cutlery 1992 silver eagle dollar with silver eagle trapper knife. Wholesale, $48.00. Retail, $90.00.

RAZORS

Cardboard sign advertising "Safety Razor," 10" high, 22" wide, $250.00 – 325.00.

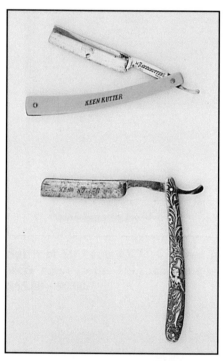

Straight razors. Top: K743, white celluloid handle with words "Keen Kutter" stamped in red, logo type letters on the front, etched in gold, full crocus polished blade, $40.00 – 60.00. Bottom: #1026, aluminum handle, hollow ground, with a woman on one side and "Keen Kutter" on other. Blade marked "Keen Kutter" and "1026 Simmons Hardware Germany," $275.00 – 350.00.

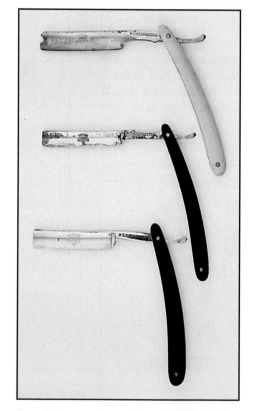

Straight razors. Top: K746 white celluloid handle, full concave blade etched in gold, full crocus polished, $30.00 – 45.00. Center: K13, gold inlaid logo, $30.00 – 45.00. Bottom: K44, plain black rubber handle, ¾ concaved blade, file tang, etched in gold, $30.00 – 45.00.

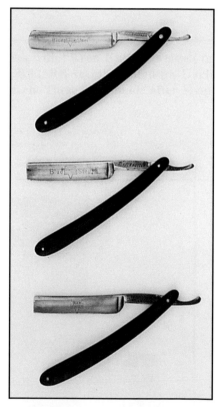

Straight razors. Top: K16, blue steel, logo in center of handle and on blade, $35.00 – 50.00. Center: K15, black handle, logo in center of handle and on blade, $35.00 – 50.00. Bottom: K15, blue steel, logo in center of handle and on blade, $35.00 – 50.00.

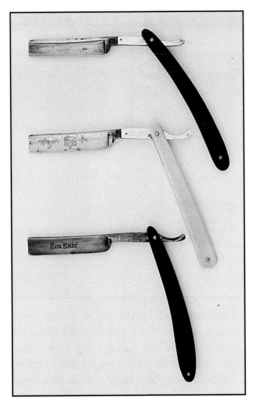

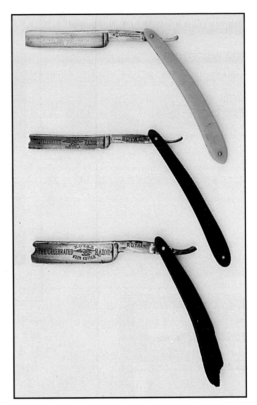

Straight razors. Top: Etched in gold on blade, mother-of-pearl on end of blade, $30.00 – 50.00. Center: #1287, mother-of-pearl on end of blade, $30.00 – 50.00. Bottom: #1150, one of the first straight razors, ⅝" blade, "Keen Kutter" written out, $25.00 – 35.00.

Straight razors, marked "Royal." Top: K419, ¾" concave blade etched in gold, $30.00 – 40.00. Center: "The Celebrated," ½" blade, $30.00 – 40.00. Bottom: "The Celebrated," ¾" blade, broken handle, $10.00 – 15.00.

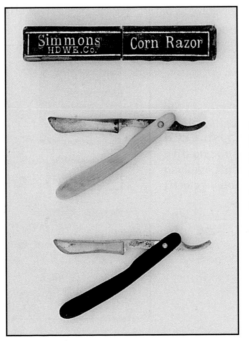

Corn razors, one with celluloid handle and one with a black rubber handle, marked Germany, $60.00 – 80.00 each; razor with the box, $100.00 – 150.00.

Straight razor boxes, top is the oldest box, prior to the logo, $15.00 – 20.00 each.

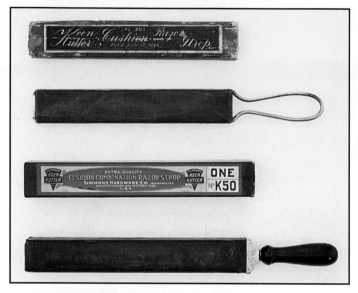

Razor strops. #205 pat. July 12, 1892, with original cover, $75.00 – 125.00; K50 cushion combination with original cover, $100.00 – 150.00.

Razor strops, E. C. Simmons, double swing: K82, $65.00 – 95.00; K81, $65.00 – 95.00; K80, $65.00 – 95.00.

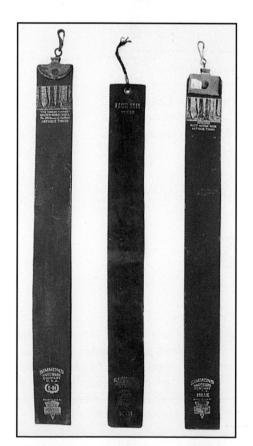

Razor strops, E. C. Simmons. K94 double swing, horse shell, $65.00 – 95.00; K711 single swing, fawn skin finish, $65.00 – 95.00; 183AK double swing, horsehide, $65.00 – 95.00.

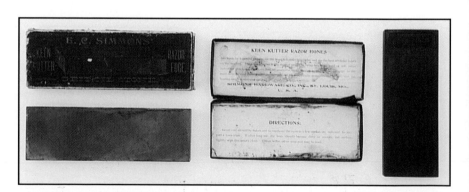

Razor hones. Left: Grit oil stone razor edge with box, $75.00 – 100.00. Right: Very old razor hone and cover has the logo in which the K makes up the first letter of both Keen and Kutter, $75.00 – 100.00.

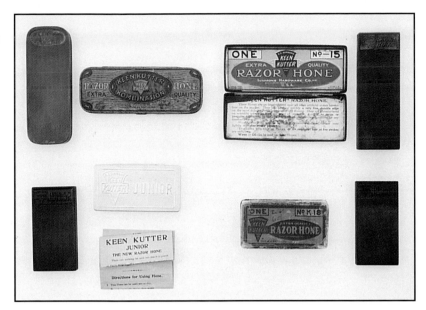

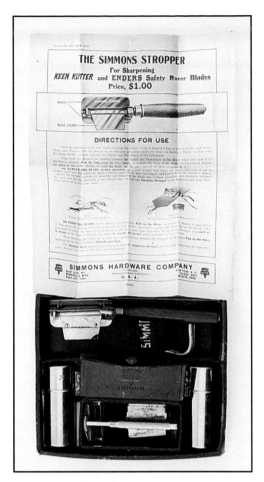

Razor hones, oil or water. K20, metal box, instructions on inside, $60.00 – 80.00; K15, cardboard box, instructions inside as shown. The outside is decorated with gold paint on black, $50.00 – 75.00; K18 Junior, aluminum box with papers, $55.00 – 75.00; K18 Junior, cardboard box, oldest version of the Junior, $55.00 – 75.00.

Junior Shaving Set with papers. The lid has the logo and words: Junior Shaving Set. It contains a stropper, blades, junior razor, stropper sharpener, and two shaving containers, $100.00 – 150.00.

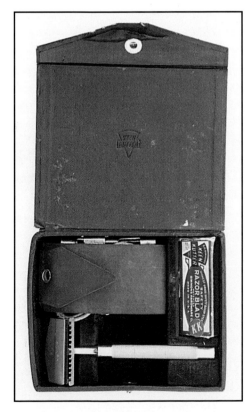

K9S safety razor display box filled with one dozen boxes of the K9S razor package shown in front of the display. Display value, $375.00 – 450.00.

Safety razor set KJ107, case is 4¼" x 3¾" x 1½". It contains the KJ107 with blade, extra pack of blades, and a K600 automatic stropper, $75.00 – 125.00.

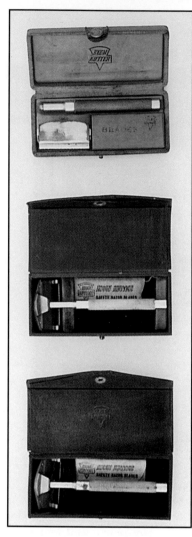

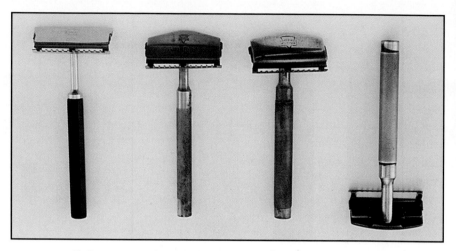

Safety razors, four different styles, $10.00 – 20.00 each.

Cardboard display for safety razor packs. The flat type lid folds down when not displayed. The box holds 20 individual boxes, each containing a safety razor, two packs of single edge blades as shown in photo, $450.00 – 550.00; individual box, $25.00.

Safety razors with metal handles in boxes. Top: Gold-plated travel kit, $50.00 – 75.00. Center: Junior safety razor, $30.00 – 40.00. Bottom: Safety razor, $30.00 – 40.00.

Safety razor with box and papers. The razor has a metal handle. Razor is Keen Kutter made by Christy Co., Fremont, Ohio, $20.00 – 30.00 set.

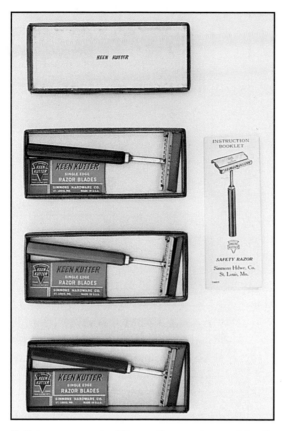

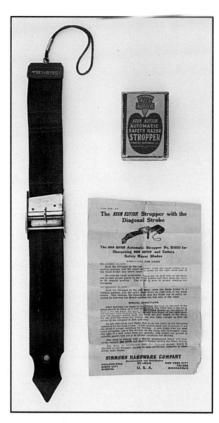

Safety razor sets. These three sets are identical except for the color of each handle. The boxes are the same color and instruction booklets are always the same as well as the blades. $25.00 – 35.00 set.

Automatic safety razor stropper, K600, in original box with instructions, Pat. 763-182. $65.00 – 85.00.

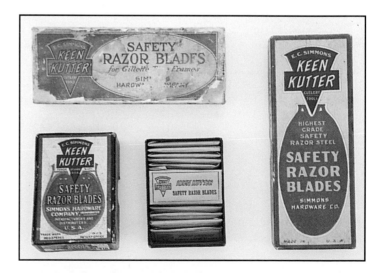

Shaving sets in containers. One container for soap or shaving stick and one container for the brush. Only one container lid was ever marked KK and it will always contain the soap or stick. The brush is marked also. $100.00 – 125.00 set.

Safety razor blades and boxes. Top: Empty box, 5¾" x 2¼", $25.00 – 35.00. Left: Box complete with 20 packs No. KIB individually wrapped blades, box, 3½" x 2½", $175.00 – 250.00 set. Right: Empty box, 6½" x 2½", held 20 packages of No. KIB safety razor blades, $35.00 – 50.00.

No. KIB single edge razor blades display. It contains the complete 20 individual packages of razor blades. Its cardboard box cover is designed to fold up for display purposes but this one has never been used. It even has the additional cardboard sleeve that the display came in. Display value, $225.00 – 300.00.

Cardboard display, 11⅜" x 12¼", with easel back, held 20 packs which are easily removed. As is, $100.00 – 125.00; complete, $225.00 – 275.00.

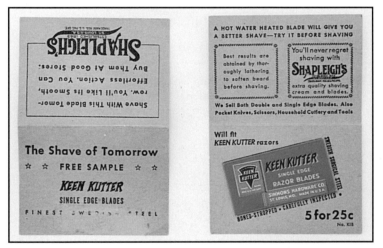

Razor samples, front and back view, they fold in half to 2¾" x 2", razor blade inside of package, $20.00 – 25.00.

Razor blade packages, all containing blades, all different, $7.50 – 15.00 each.

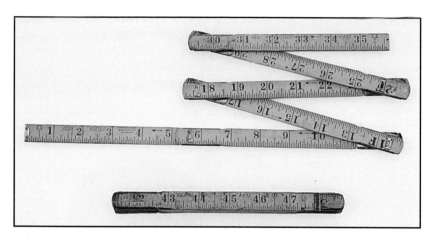

Folding zig-zag rules. Top: K603, 3' six-fold enameled yellow with several patent dates on it, $175.00 – 250.00. Bottom: K504, 4' eight-fold enameled yellow with Pat. June 5, 1900, $175.00 – 250.00.

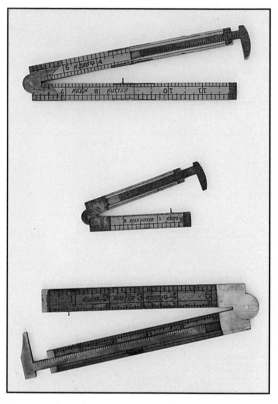

Boxwood caliper rules. Top: K320, 1' four-fold, 1" wide, folded, $95.00 – 125.00 mint. Center: K360, 6" two-fold, unbound, ⅞" wide, folded, $95.00 – 125.00 mint. Bottom: K360½, 1" two-fold, unbound, 1⅜" wide, folded, $65.00 – 85.00.

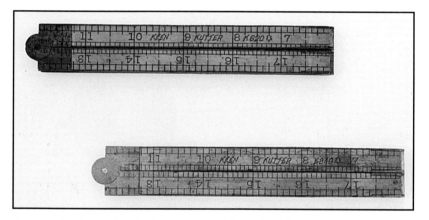

Boxwood rules, folded. Top: K620, 2' four-fold, brass bound, 1" wide, $65.00 – 85.00. Bottom: K840, 2' four-fold, half-bound brass, 1" wide, $50.00 – 75.00.

Boxwood rules, all unbound and folded. Top: K680, 2' four-fold, 1" wide, $35.00 – 55.00. Center: K660½, 3' four-fold, 1" wide, $50.00 – 75.00. Bottom: K610, 2' four-fold, 1" wide, $35.00 – 45.00; K690, 1' four-fold, ⅝" wide, $35.00 – 50.00.

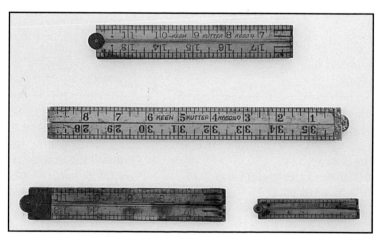

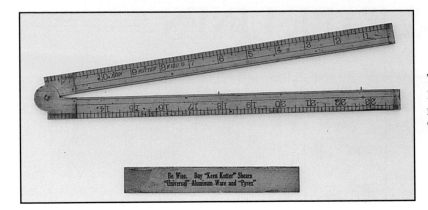

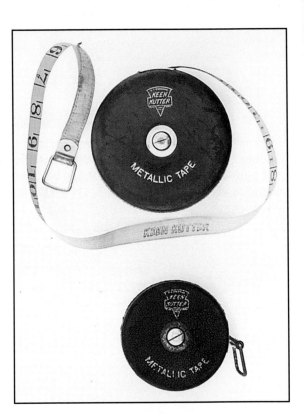

Top: Boxwood rule, K180, two-fold, 2' unbound, 1½'' wide, folded, $65.00 – 85.00. Bottom: Wooden ruler, 6'', advertising Keen Kutter shears, $50.00 – 75.00.

Metallic tape lines with "Keen Kutter" written on tape. Top: K52, 50', $50.00 – 75.00. Bottom: K51, 25', $70.00 – 100.00.

Steel tape lines with Keen Kutter written on tape. Top: K62, 50', $50.00 – 75.00. Center: Junior steel tape, 100', $50.00 – 75.00. Bottom: Junior steel tape, 25', $70.00 – 100.00.

Top: F5006GK tape line, one of Shapleigh's last, made by Lufkin, has a Lufkin tape in it, $75.00 – 100.00. Bottom: K73 E. C. Simmons tape line, has "E. C. Simmons" written on the tape, $100.00 – 150.00.

E. C. Simmons 50' metallic cloth tape line in original box, K52. $275.00 – 325.00 set.

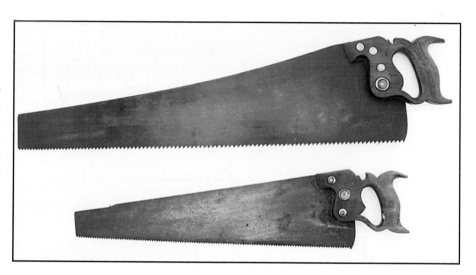

Hand saws, E. C. Simmons, buttons have the axe head with "Keen Kutter" written around it. Top: 28" blade with "Keen Kutter" written fancy on the blade, $50.00 – 75.00. Bottom: 20" blade, has nib and fancy marked blade, $50.00 – 75.00.

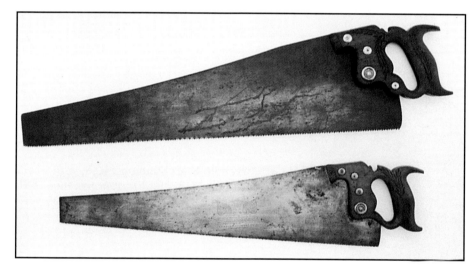

Hand saws, E. C. Simmons both have fancy flag designs on the blade. Top: 26" blade, button has the axe head with "Keen Kutter" written around it, $50.00 – 75.00. Bottom: 22" blade No. 88, $75.00 – 125.00.

Hand saws, logo and wording still on blade. K24, E. C. Simmons, 26" blade, $50.00 – 75.00; K18 with logo button, 26" blade, $50.00 – 75.00. If blade lettering is not legible, $10.00.

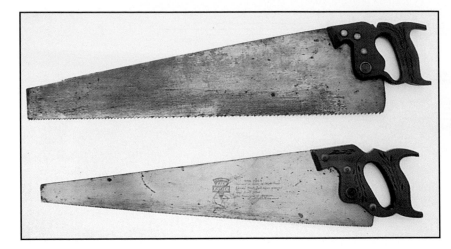

Hand saws, E. C. Simmons, with logo, markings, and wording still on blades. K816, 28" blade, logo button, $50.00 – 75.00; K726S, 26" blade, marked button, $50.00 – 75.00.

Hand saw, E. C. Simmons, No. 88, has fancy flags and writing on 22" blade. Button has axe head with "Keen Kutter" written around it, $75.00 – 125.00.

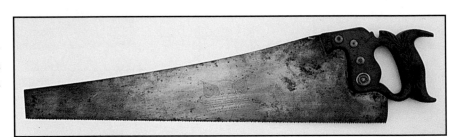

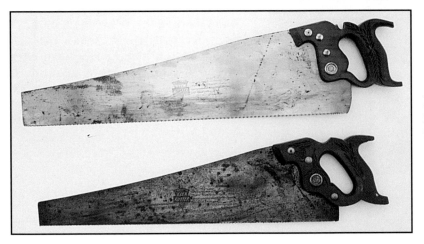

Hand saws, both E. C. Simmons, K88, with wording and logo on blades and button has logo. 22", $50.00 – 75.00; 20", $50.00 – 75.00.

Hand saws, both E. C. Simmons, K88, wording and logo on blades, button has logo. 18", $50.00 – 75.00; 16", $50.00 – 75.00.

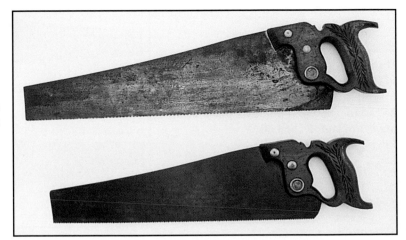

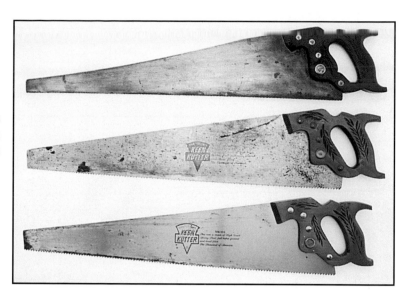

Hand saws, all K88S, 26" blades. Top: E. C. Simmons with button logo, $10.00 – 20.00. Next two: Shapleigh with wording on blades, button has logo. One is newer than the other. $50.00 – 75.00 each.

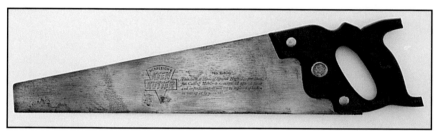

Metal cutting saw, Shapleigh K106, 15 teeth per inch, 18" blade, wording still on blade, $85.00 – 100.00.

Top: Flooring saw, adjustable, logo on 18" blade, $175.00 – 200.00. Bottom: KK6 stair builder's saw, steel blade, applewood handle, 6" blade, logo on blade. This one is mint condition, $200.00 – 250.00.

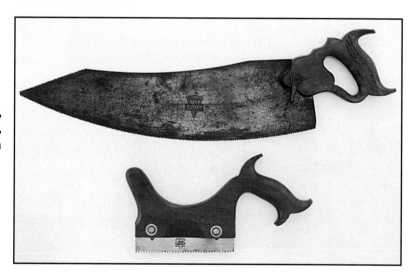

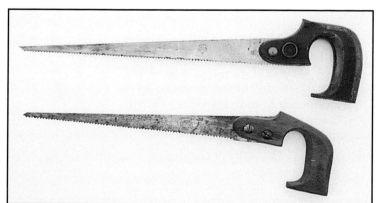

Compass saws. Top: Shapleigh 14" blade, logo button, $25.00 – 35.00. Bottom: E. C. Simmons 10" blade, $35.00 – 50.00.

Iron pad keyhole saw, 4¼" long iron handle, Pat Aug 28, 1877, 7" blade is reversible and butt end forms a screwdriver blade, $50.00 – 75.00.

Top: E. C. Simmons adjustable and reversible combined panel and back saw, 16" blade with logo on blade, pat. Jan'y 9-06, $125.00 – 150.00. Center: K44 back saw with 12" blade, $40.00 – 60.00. Bottom: K44 back saw with 10" blade, $40.00 – 60.00.

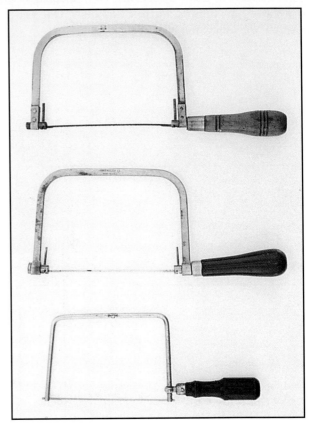

Coping saws. Top: K50, heavy pattern with logo, $20.00 – 30.00. Center: K50, heavy pattern with Keen Kutter written out, both have a 6½" blade but adjust to take a 6" blade, $20.00 – 30.00. Bottom: 6" blade, notched at both ends so that blades can be faced up or down either side, $40.00 – 60.00.

Coping saw blades. Box only for one gross, KB6½, $35.00 – 45.00; package of one dozen, KB6½, $30.00 – 40.00; full box of one gross KC6 blades (package inside unmarked as shown), $50.00 – 75.00; package of 10 K6½P blades, $20.00 – 30.00.

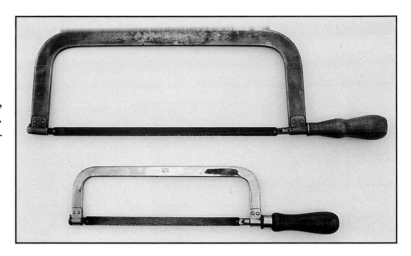

Hack saws. Top: for 12" blades, overall length 20", extra heavy and not adjustable, $55.00 – 70.00. Bottom: K188, not adjustable for 8" blade, $55.00 – 70.00.

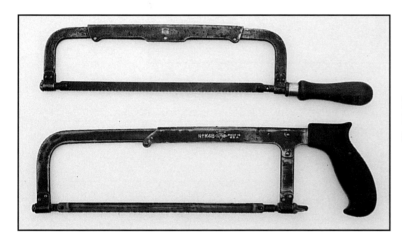

Hack saws. Top: K188A adjustable for 8" to 12" blades, $35.00 – 45.00. Bottom: K48 adjustable "pistol grip" to fit 8" to 12" blades, $35.00 – 45.00.

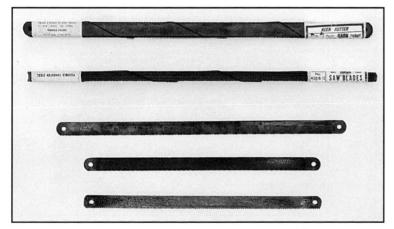

Hack saw blades. Unused packages containing one dozen, $125.00 – 175.00 per package; individual blades, $10.00 – 15.00 each.

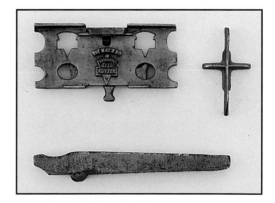

No. K, complete set of saw tools comprising a combined raker tooth gauge, jointer, side file, setting block, and tooth set gauge, $35.00 – 50.00.

Saw clamp, folding pattern, overall length 12", width 3", $150.00 – 200.00. Saw in the saw clamp shown below.

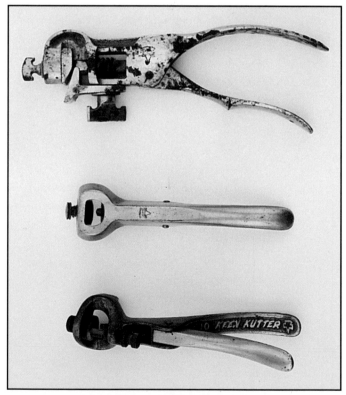

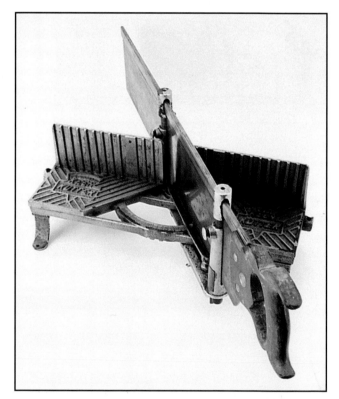

Saw sets. Top: Wide tooth style used for cross cut saw, $40.00 – 50.00. Center: K10 dial pattern with revolving anvil, "Keen Kutter" written in handle, logo on handle and top, $18.00 – 30.00. Bottom: "Keen Kutter" written on inside of handle, logo on top, $18.00 – 30.00.

Miter box, complete with saw, $275.00 – 350.00.

Display, cardboard easel back sign advertising scissors and shears, 21" x 24". Shown holding a pair of scissors. $300.00 – 350.00.

Shears and scissors showcase, missing the rotating rack in the center to hang scissors on. This one has wood on all four glass corners, 15¾" base x 16¾" x 31" tall, $500.00 – 700.00; complete with rack, $1,000.00 – 1,200.00.

Shears and scissors showcase with rotating rack in the center to hang scissors on, 15¾" base x 14½" x 31" tall, $1,000.00 – 1,200.00.

Cardboard easel type advertisement for shears as Christmas gifts, 9" x 6", $75.00 – 100.00.

Colorful cardboard boxes for scissors and shears, $25.00 – 45.00 each.

Three-piece scissor sets in leather cases, $100.00 – 150.00 each.

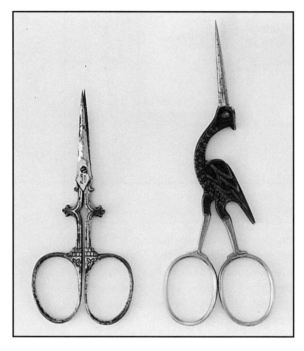

Left: 3½" embroidery scissors, fancy, $35.00 – 50.00. Right: 4" stork pattern scissors, $175.00 – 225.00.

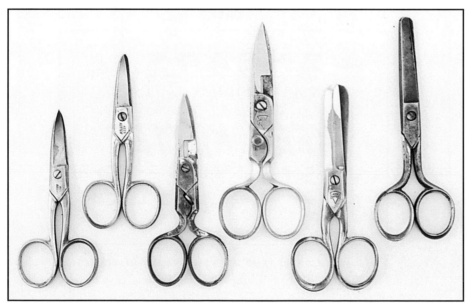

Left to right: 4" nail scissors with round bows, $10.00 – 20.00; 4" nail scissors with round bows, $10.00 – 20.00; 4¾" buttonhole scissors, Germany, $30.00 – 50.00; 5" buttonhole scissors, Germany, $30.00 – 50.00; 4½" pocket scissors, $8.00 – 15.00; 5½" pocket scissors, Germany, $8.00 – 15.00.

Cardboard box containing original S128AK scissor, $75.00 – 100.00.

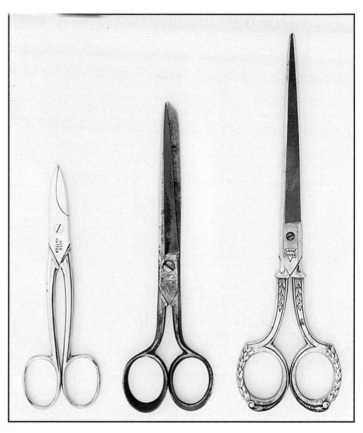

Left to right: 5½" medical scissors, marked Germany, $20.00 – 25.00; 7" ladies or regular scissors, $8.00 – 12.00; 8½" scissors with fancy handles, $50.00 – 75.00.

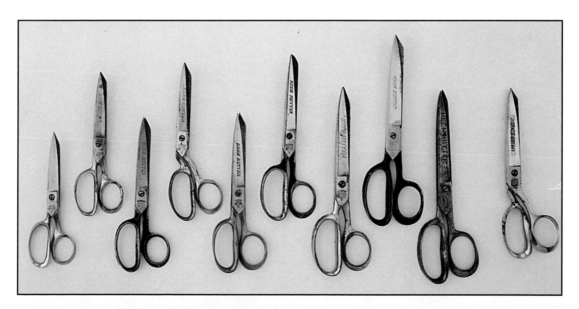

Left to right: 5½" scissors, $8.00 – 12.00 each; 6" scissors, $8.00 – 12.00 each; 6½" black handled scissors, $8.00 – 12.00 each; 6½" bent style scissors, $8.00 – 12.00 each; 7" scissors, $8.00 – 12.00 each; 7" black handled scissors, $8.00 – 12.00 each; 8" scissors, $8.00 – 12.00 each; 8" black handled scissors, $8.00 – 12.00 each; 8" scissors, old version, with patent date and "Keen Kutter" written out, $8.00 – 12.00; 7" scissors, double stamped, marked "Diamond Edge" and "Keen Kutter," $25.00 – 30.00.

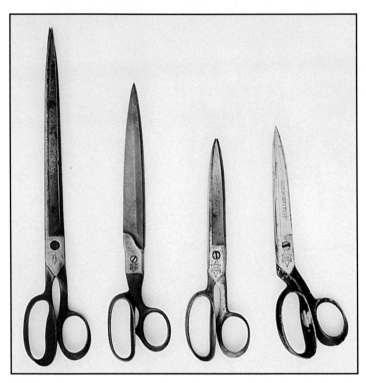

Desk, paper or bankers shears, left one has Keen Kutter written out, next has logo, $20.00 – 30.00 each; two pairs of 10'' shears, $10.00 – 15.00 each.

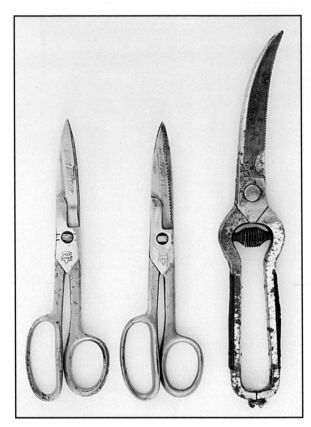

Left to right: Kitchen shears, two different, $15.00 – 18.00 each; game carving shears, 10¼'' with serrated edge and bone cutter on lower blade, $50.00 – 75.00.

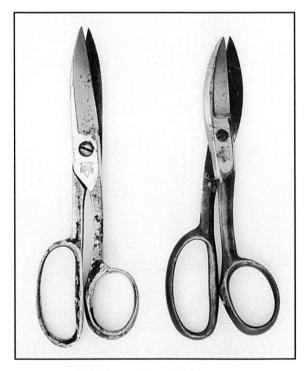

Dental snips: K11D 7½'', $15.00 – 20.00; dental or factory snips, 7'', $15.00 – 20.00.

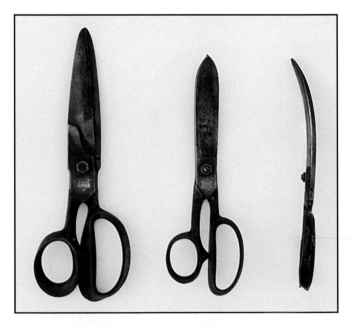

Mule shears, 10½'', $20.00 – 30.00; roaching shears, 9'' and 9¼'', $20.00 – 30.00 each.

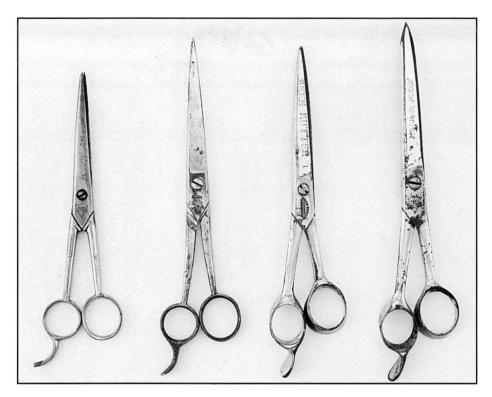

Barber's shears, 7", $15.00 – 25.00; 7½" Germany, $15.00 – 25.00; 7½", old version with patent date, $15.00 – 25.00; 8½", $15.00 – 25.00.

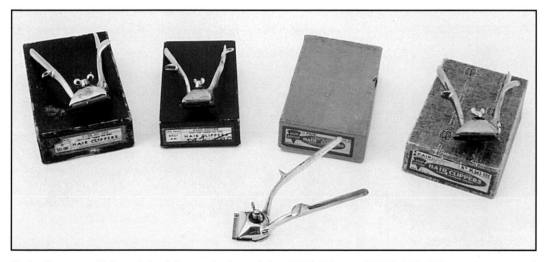

Hair clippers, all in original boxes. Left to right: S521AK, two K543-000 different boxes, and K538-00, $35.00 – 45.00 each.

SCREWDRIVERS

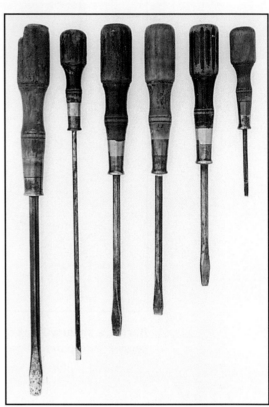

Screwdriver display rack, 24'' long x 10½'' high x 5½'' wide, $125.00 – 175.00.

Screwdrivers with wood handles and brass ferrules. Blade sizes range from 2½'' to 9'', $30.00 – 40.00 each.

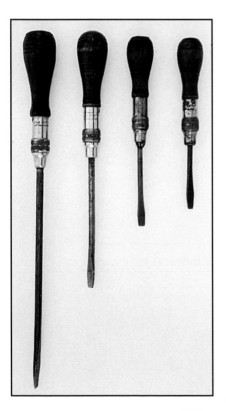

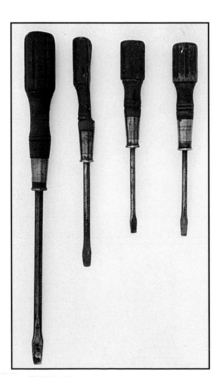

Left:
Screwdrivers, ratchet, adjust to work with right and left hand ratchet or rigid, each has patent date 12-13-1892. Top of each handle has a brass logo. Blade sizes 10'', 6'', 4'', and 3'', $75.00 – 100.00 each.

Right:
Screwdrivers, brass ferrules. Blade sizes left to right: 8'', $40.00 – 50.00; 5'', $35.00 – 45.00; 4'', $35.00 – 45.00; 4'', marked "Special," $40.00 – 50.00.

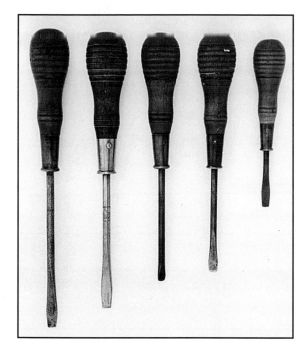

Screwdrivers, beaded hardwood handles. Blade sizes, left to right: 5½", marked Blue Brand, $20.00 – 30.00; 5", marked Blue Brand, $20.00 – 30.00; 4", $20.00 – 30.00; 3¾", $20.00 – 30.00; 2", $20.00 – 30.00.

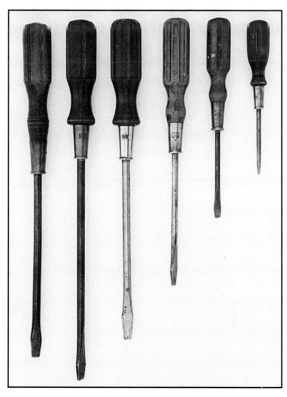

Screwdrivers with steel ferrules through hardwood handles. Blades range from 3" to 10", $20.00 – 30.00 each.

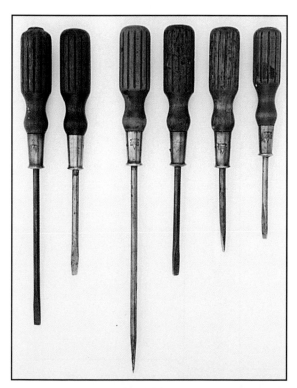

Cabinet screwdrivers with hardwood handles, slender blades, and fine points. These have steel through entire handle. Blade sizes from 3" to 7½", $20.00 – 30.00 each.

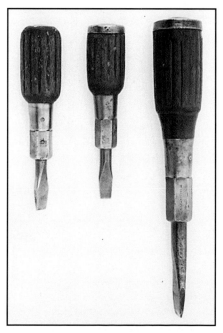

Machinist's screwdrivers, steel blade extends through handle, steel ferrule. Patent date 9-24-03. Overall lengths: 5¼", 5½", and 8¾", $30.00 – 35.00 each.

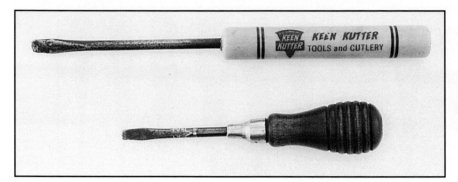

Top: Screwdriver, advertising for Marion, IL, $75.00 – 100.00. Bottom: Screwdriver for sewing machine, $75.00 – 125.00.

Offset screwdriver for use in cramped places No. K7, overall length 6¾", $65.00 – 85.00.

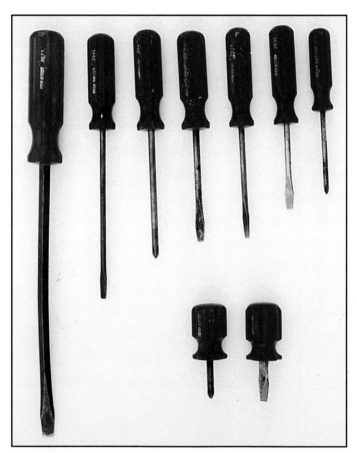

Screwdrivers with tenite plastic handles. Top shows both Phillips and regulars, all have numbers stamped in white in the handle, $8.00 – 15.00 each. Bottom two are called "Stubby," $8.00 – 15.00 each.

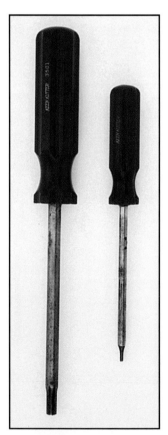

Screwdrivers, torx tip, tenite plastic handles, KPA3, blade size 4½", $10.00 – 15.00; 3501, blade size 6", $10.00 – 15.00.

SHOWCASES

Left:
Showcase, slant top, opens from back, logo etched in glass on top left hand corner, 14" x 20", $400.00 – 500.00.

Right:
Outside display case for pocket cutlery, razors, scissors and shears. It is 41" high x 6"wide x 7" deep with an etched glass front and two glass sides, $800.00 – 1,200.00.

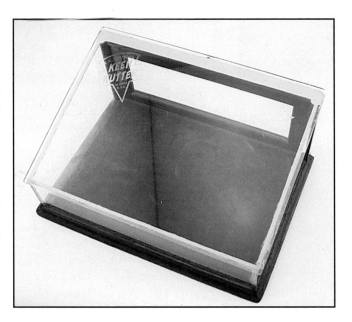

Showcase for displaying cutlery, 36" x 24" x 12" high, $700.00 – 900.00.

Showcase for displaying cutlery, 53½" x 28" x 17" high, contains spaces for 54 patterns of pocket knives, 12 patterns of scissors and shears, and four patterns for razors. This is the case designed for the knife and shear boxes, $800.00 – 1,200.00.

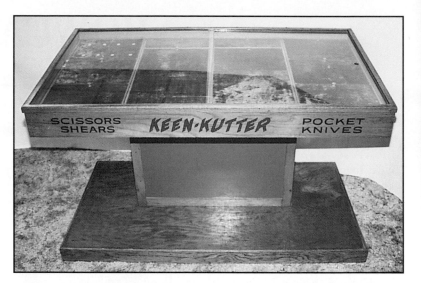

Modern merchandiser slant top showcase, 57" long x 31¼" wide x 32⅛" high in front, and 35" high in back, complete with four felt-lined with buttons, lift-up panels under which is storage area for open stock. Top consists of two large sections of sliding glass, $700.00 – 1,000.00.

Showcase, 33" base, 33" tall, has curved glass. Etched on the glasses are items it displayed, fine Hornet pocket knives, Keen Kutter scissors, Keen Kutter shears, and Keen Kutter pocket knives, $1,750.00 – 2,100.00.

Showcase, called 6', 24" deep x 42" high x 72" long, two Keen Kutter logos etched in the glass, $1,200.00 – 1,700.00. Showcase, 8' (not pictured) with two Keen Kutter logos etched in the glass, $1,000.00 – 1,500.00.

Top:
This bronze name plate was originally mounted on a K200 scissors and shear merchandise case. The complete case was brought to me before I became a serious Keen Kutter collector. I purchased it just for the name plate and told the seller to do whatever he wanted with the case. The case was 29¾" x 11½" x 3½" front, 8" back, slant top per catalog. Name plate, 12" x 1½", $300.00 – 400.00.

Bottom: Double-sided wooden "Silent Salesman" rack, top size 6" x 59", $75.00 – 100.00.

SQUARES

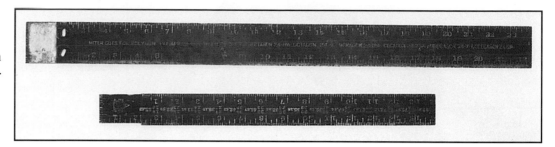

Square, Take Down #KT100, $225.00 – 275.00.

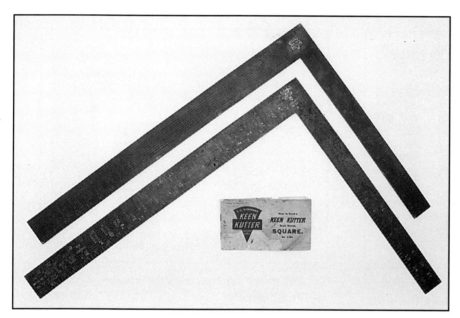

Square, KF100, E. C. Simmons, $25.00 – 35.00; Square, No. KF, patent 1-22-01, $25.00 – 35.00; book, *How To Read A Keen Kutter Square*, $50.00 – 75.00.

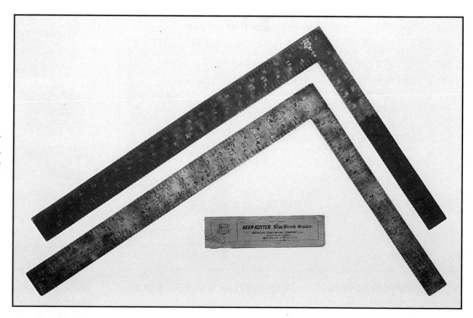

Square, KC3, copper finish, $25.00 – 35.00; square, K3, Blue Brand, $25.00 – 35.00; book, *How to Read a Blue Brand Square*, $50.00 – 75.00.

Square, K18, tongue length 12", $40.00 – 50.00. Square, K10, tongue length 8", $50.00 – 75.00.

Tri squares with wooden handles and logo on the blade. 9", $40.00 – 60.00; 6", $40.00 – 60.00; 4½", $40.00 – 60.00.

Tri and miter squares, wooden handles with logo on the blade. Pat. April 27, '09, 7½", $40.00 – 60.00; 6", $40.00 – 60.00.

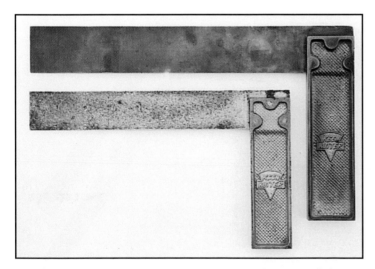

Tri squares with steel handles, logo on handles, 10", $45.00 – 65.00; 8", $35.00 – 50.00.

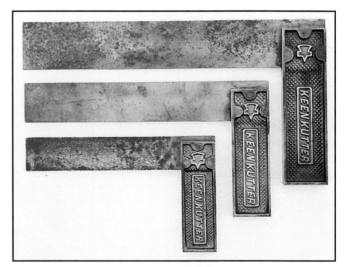

Tri squares, steel handles with Keen Kutter written out on the handle and logo above. 10", $45.00 – 65.00; 8", $35.00 – 50.00; 6", $35.00 – 50.00.

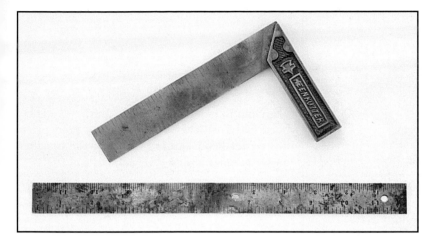

Square tri and miter, 6" blade with cast iron handle with "Keen Kutter" written out and logo above, $35.00 – 50.00; K312 steel rule, 12", $65.00 – 85.00.

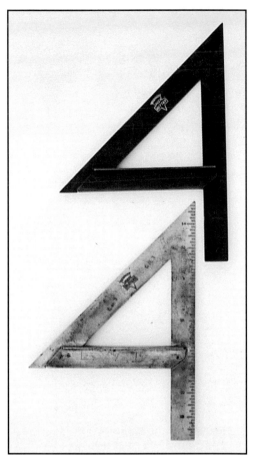

Miter 10" four squares, one black japenning and one nickel plated, $75.00 – 100.00 each.

Sliding T-bevel squares, wood handles with logo on blades, 6", $50.00 – 75.00; 8", $40.00 – 55.00; 10", $40.00 – 55.00.

Sliding T-bevel squares with cast iron handles with Keen Kutter written out and logo on top. 6", $70.00 – 90.00; 8", $40.00 – 60.00; 10", $40.00 – 60.00.

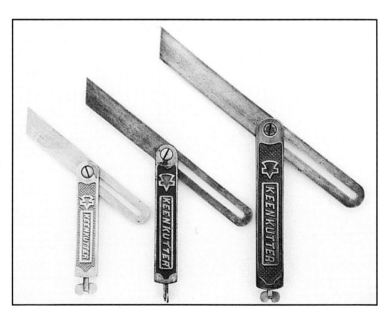

Combination square, maroon finish, 9" blade, head fitted with level and scribing point, also has center head and bevel protractor that fits on the blade, $250.00 – 275.00.

Combination squares marked on blade, always have a maroon handle, 12", $75.00 – 100.00; 9", $125.00 – 150.00.

MISCELLANEOUS TOOLS

Plumb bob, 16 oz., $175.00 – 200.00; plumb bob, K50, 4½ oz. with original box, $250.00 – 325.00.

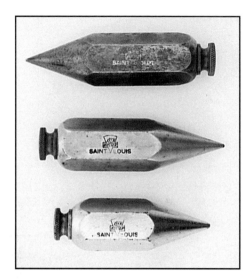

Plumb bobs, hexagon shape, two different 7 oz. and one 6 oz., $75.00 – 125.00 each.

Lubricator, No. KL, round oil can with screw top and squirt nozzle, 6¼" tall x 2½" diameter, ½-pint. For lawn mowers, bicycles, jig saws, and sewing machines, $175.00 – 200.00.

Plumb bobs, hexagon shape, still have original red paint, sizes 8 oz. and 3 oz., $75.00 – 125.00 each.

Oil bottle, K114, with oil still in it, paper label, with original cardboard box, $175.00 – 225.00.

Oil bottles, glass, small blue, 4" tall x 1½", $50.00 – 75.00; large blue, 5½" tall x 2", $75.00 – 95.00.

Oil bottles, clear, 5½", $75.00 – 95.00; 4", $50.00 – 75.00.

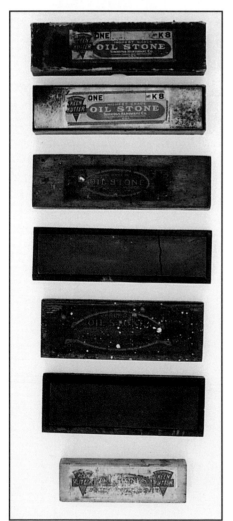

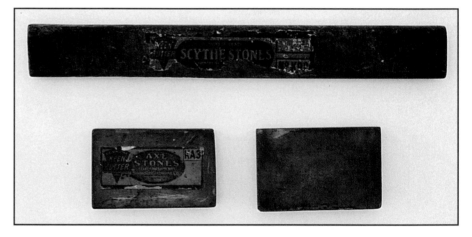

Scythe stone, 10" x 1½", $75.00 – 100.00; axe stones, 3" x 2", one is a KA3, the other has the old shield emblem, $75.00 – 100.00 each.

Oil stones, K8 with cardboard box, $125.00 – 200.00; KM8, mounted in wooden box, $125.00 – 200.00; KCM72 mounted in wooden box, $125.00 – 200.00; K6 without box, $50.00 – 100.00.

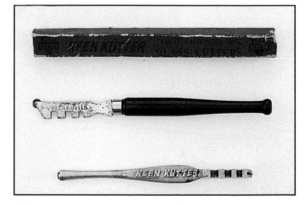

Glass cutter with black handle and original box, $100.00 – 125.00; glass cutter with "Keen Kutter" written on handle, $40.00 – 50.00.

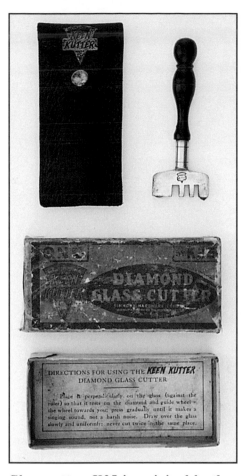

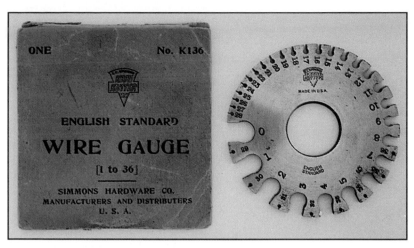

Wire gauge with original paper pouch, K136, $350.00 – 450.00.

Glass cutter, K25 in original leather pouch containing a gold logo, with the original box. $225.00 – 250.00; without box, $125.00 – 150.00.

Hand grinder, 7" wheel, $175.00 – 225.00.

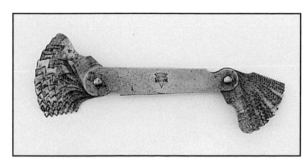

Screw pitch gauge, each leaf is stamped showing the pitch, $250.00 – 300.00.

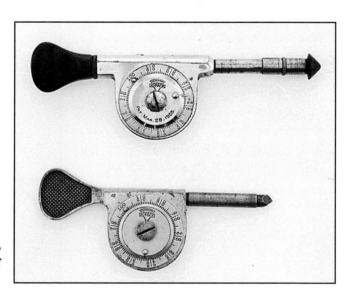

Speed indicators, one has Pat. Mar 28, 1905, used to find speed of revolving axles or spindles of any kind of machinery, $100.00 – 150.00 each.

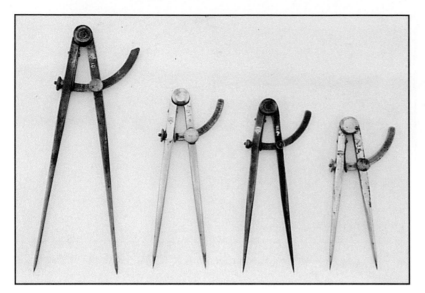

Dividers. 6", $40.00 – 50.00; 7", $40.00 – 50.00; 8", $40.00 – 50.00; 10", $40.00 – 50.00.

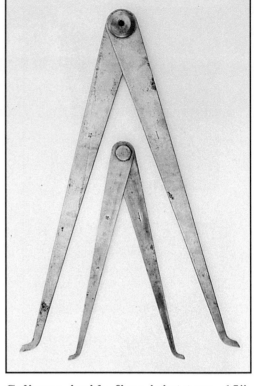

Calipers, inside firm joint type. 15", $50.00 – 75.00; 9", $50.00 – 75.00.

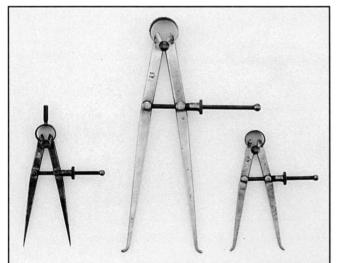

K64, 4" divider, strong steel string type, $40.00 – 50.00; K28, 8" inside calipers, $40.00 – 50.00; K24, 4" inside calipers, $45.00 – 50.00.

Calipers, outside. K38, 8", $40.00 – 50.00; K36, 6", $40.00 – 50.00; K34, 4", $50.00 – 75.00.

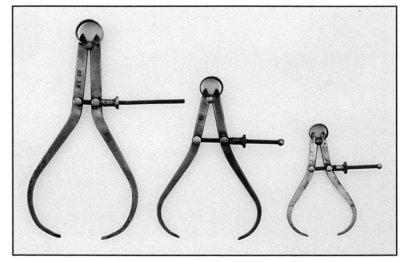

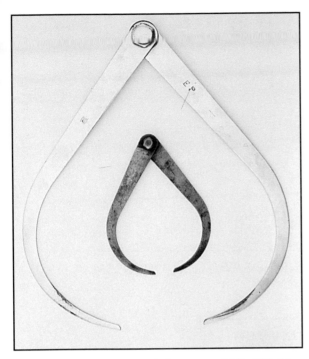

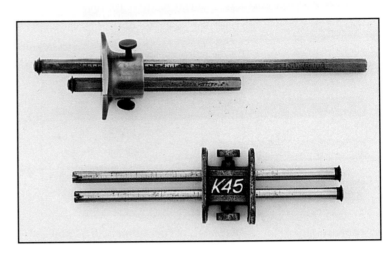

Marking gauges, metal. Double roller, one bar 8¼", other 4", $100.00 – 150.00; K45 double roller, overall length 7", $90.00 – 125.00.

Calipers, outside firm joint type. 12", $50.00 – 75.00; 6", $50.00 – 75.00.

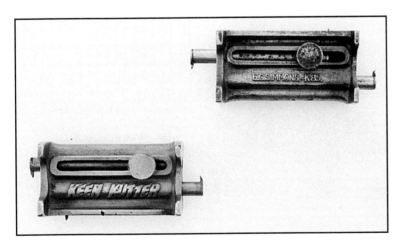

Butt gauges, K85, E. C. Simmons, showing markings on both sides, $75.00 – 95.00 each.

Carpenter pencils, set of twelve, still has the cardboard sleeve around them, unused, mint, $300.00 – 375.00.

Marking gauges, wooden. Top to bottom: 8" rosewood with two brass strips in head, $60.00 – 90.00; 8" beechwood with two brass strips in head, $35.00 – 50.00; K25 graduated in 16ths for 6", $30.00 – 50.00; 8" with oval head, $30.00 – 50.00.

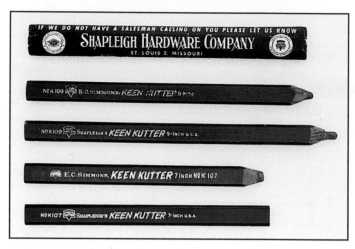

Cardboard sleeve for a Shapleigh carpenter pencil, $75.00 – 95.00. Various carpenter pencils: used, $10.00 – 15.00; unused, $15.00 – 20.00.

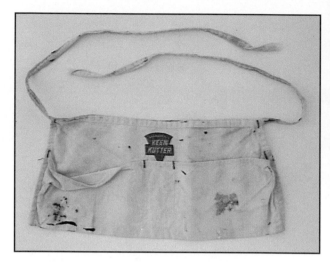

Nail apron, two pocket, 17" x 8", $50.00 – 75.00.

Nail apron, cloth, Shapleigh, 21½" x 16", $90.00 – 110.00.

Box or crate openers, each has one checked and one smooth face. 7½" with logo, $100.00 – 150.00; 9" with logo, $100.00 – 125.00; 9" with "Keen Kutter" written out, $100.00 – 125.00.

Tack claws, all are K5 and 7" long with different markings on the blades, $20.00 – 25.00.

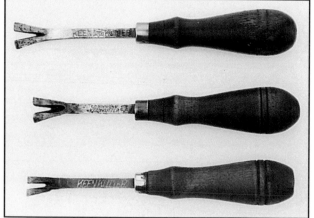

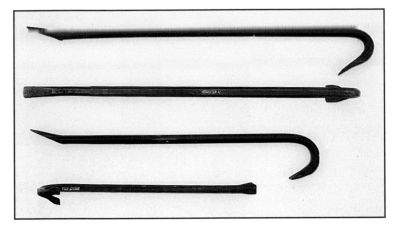

Carpenter wrecking bars, goose neck. 30", $50.00 – 65.00; 28", $50.00 – 65.00; 24", $50.00 – 65.00; 18", $50.00 – 65.00.

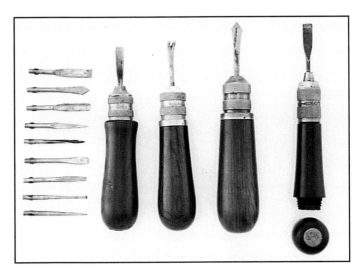

Awl and tool sets, complete with tools. The tools have ears which fit in the jaws and tighten by the chuck. When not in use, the tools are stored in the handle around the post by the chuck, $50.00 – 85.00.

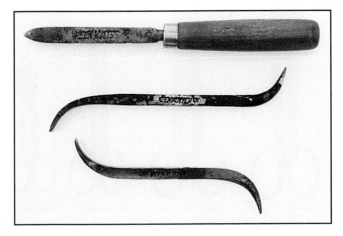

Top: Bearing scraper, $50.00 – 75.00. Center and bottom: Cotter pin lifter and spreader combination, $40.00 – 60.00 each.

Nail pullers, two different, 18", $45.00 – 65.00 each.

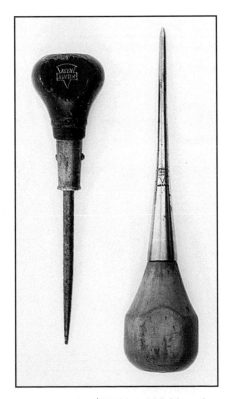

Scratch awls, $75.00 – 125.00 each.

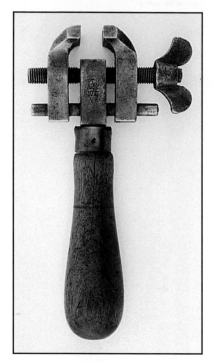

Hand screw, adjustable jaws, length 10", arrow points to logo on both sides, $75.00 – 125.00.

Hand vise, K49, 7" long, removable pin which can be driven out and vise used in a brace, $175.00 – 225.00.

Wire brush, F1816H, $50.00 – 75.00.

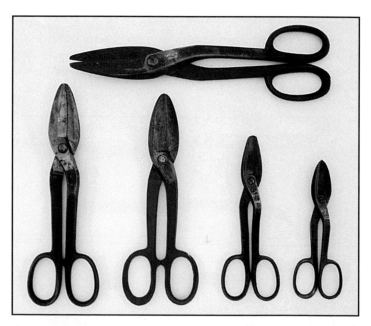

Leather punches, four different types: $18.00 – 22.00 each. Revolving four-tube #K44 punch with tube's numbers 4, 6, 8 and 10, $45.00 – 65.00.

Top: Combination circular/straight tinner's snips with "Keen Kutter" written out. Bottom: Various types of tinner's snips with logos, $25.00 – 35.00 each.

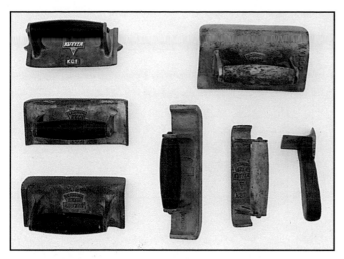

Cement sidewalk tools, Nos. KO100, K017, K02, K01, K038, and K037. Some are edgers and jointers, all are handled, $125.00 – 150.00 each. Far right: radius tool, $125.00 – 150.00.

Linoleum knives, various sizes, $15.00 – 20.00 each.

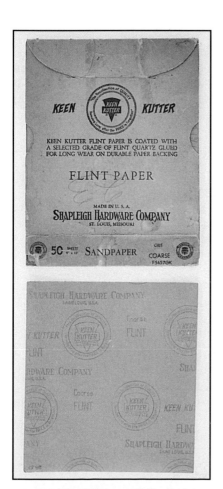

Emery cloth, blue for steel sanding, $25.00 – 30.00; flint or sandpaper, two sheets, $25.00 – 50.00 each.

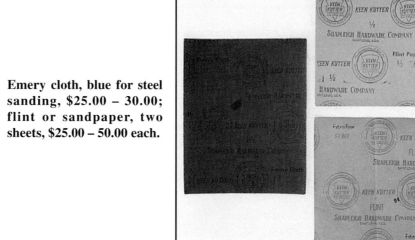

Flint or sandpaper pack containing 50 sheets of coarse, $100.00 – 125.00 package alone; individual sheet of F54576K coarse, $25.00 – 50.00.

Putty or scraping knives, variety, $15.00 – 35.00 each.

TOOL BOXES

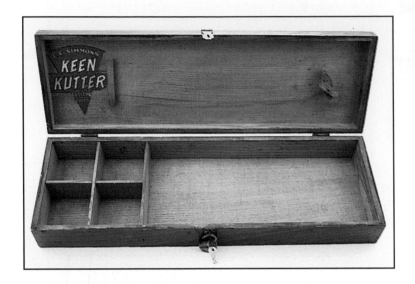

Tool box for tool set No. K1. Still has the original logo and paperwork showing contents, original lock and key. Size is 27½" x 9" x 5". The photos show it empty, filled, and closed with paperwork. Value of box and paperwork without tools, $450.00 – 550.00.

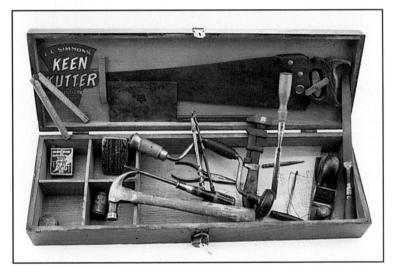

Canvas tool bag, K20, folding steel frame, leather covered, 20" x 6" x 16" deep, $175.00 – 225.00.

Leather tool box, logo stamped in leather. As is, $100.00 – 150.00; with original decals on the inside and in good condition, $300.00 – 350.00.

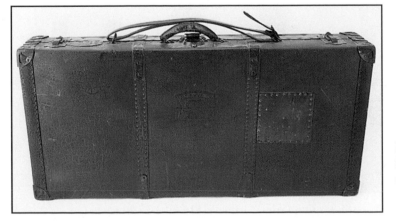

Oak wall-hung tool cabinet, 19" wide x 27½" tall x 8" deep, has original decals, without tools, $450.00 – 650.00.

Oak wall-hung double-door tool cabinet, 22½" wide x 31" tall x 8" deep, $500.00 – 750.00 (without tools).

Tool gift set, includes Keen Kutter push drill, hammer, screwdriver, and pliers in a black case, $1,000.00.

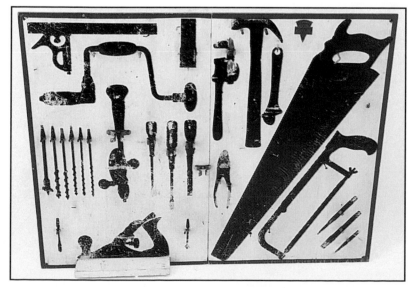

Folding tool display board that has outlines of tools, 18" x 28" when folded, $75.00 – 100.00.

WRENCHES

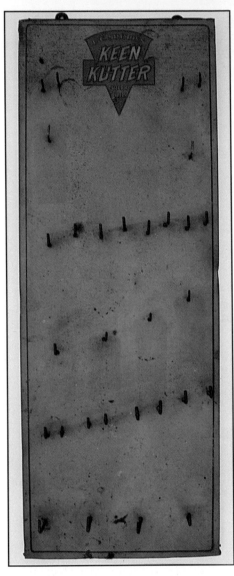

Wrench assortment display board #K30A. It came with one dozen Keen Kutter general purpose and 1½ dozen Keen Kutter textile and machine wrenches. Without the wrenches, $350.00 – 450.00.

General purpose wrenches, "Keen Kutter" written on end, $25.00 – 35.00 each. Left to right: K1000, 7/16'' and 1/2''; K750, 3/8'' and 7/16''; K580, 5/16'' and 3/8''; K500, 1/4'' and 5/16''.

Keen Kutter general purpose wrenches in roll, complete with five wrenches, one of each Nos. K380, K500, K580, K750, and K1000. $500.00 – 750.00.

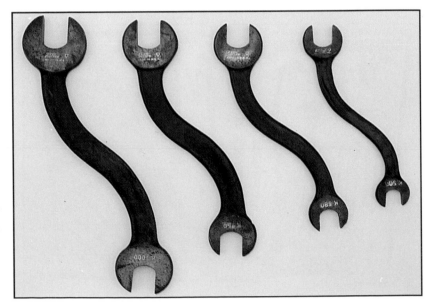

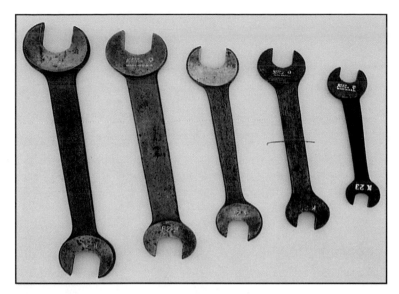

Engineer's wrenches, $25.00 – 35.00. Left to right: K31, ⁷⁄₁₆'' and ½''; K29, ³⁄₈'' and ⁷⁄₁₆''; K27, ⁵⁄₁₆'' and ³⁄₈''; K25, ¼'' and ⁵⁄₁₆''; K23, ³⁄₁₆'' and ¼''.

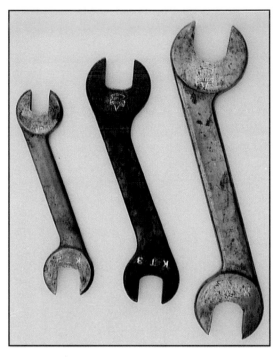

Textile and machine wrenches with logo, $35.00 – 45.00 each. KT2, ³⁄₁₆'' and ¼''; KT3, ¼'' and ⁵⁄₁₆''; KT5, ³⁄₈'' and ⁷⁄₁₆''.

Tappet wrenches, $30.00 – 40.00 each. Top: K1, ⁷⁄₁₆'' and ½''. Bottom: K2, ⁹⁄₁₆'' and ⁵⁄₈''.

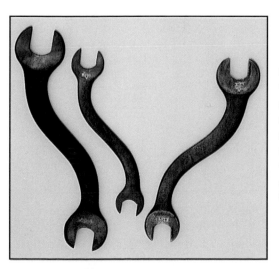

General purpose wrenches with logo, $35.00 – 45.00 each. These wrenches were manufactured at various times and show the logo on different sides of the wrenches. Left: K750, ³⁄₈'' and ⁷⁄₁₆''; K500, ¼'' and ⁵⁄₁₆''; K580, ³⁄₈'' and ⁵⁄₁₆''.

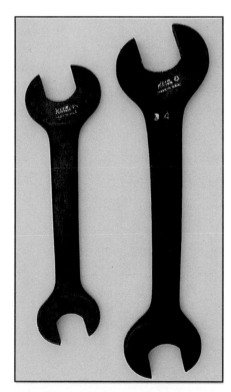

Engineer's wrenches, $30.00 – 40.00 each. Left: K31, ⁷⁄₁₆'' and ½''. Right: K34, ½'' and ⁵⁄₈''.

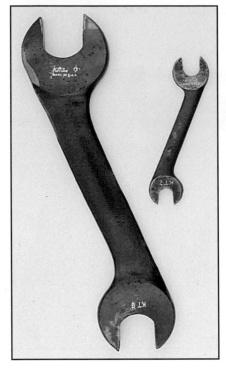

Textile and machine wrenches. Left: KT9, ⅝" and ¾", $50.00 – 60.00. Right: KT2, ³⁄₁₆" and ¼", $25.00 – 35.00.

Alligator wrenches, combination bolt wrenches. Left to right: (numbers appear on backs of wrenches) K12, $40.00 – 60.00; K20, natural finish, $40.00 – 60.00; K30, nickel plated, $40.00 – 60.00; K40, $40.00 – 60.00; K50, $50.00 – 75.00.

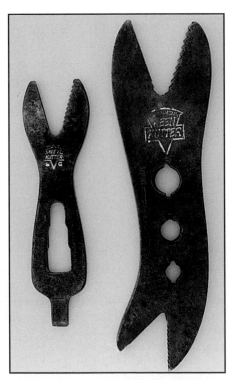

Adjustable alligator wrench, patent date: 5-26-03, $100.00 – 150.00.

Left: K15 combination bolt wrench with screwdriver end, $65.00 – 80.00. Right: K23 combination bolt wrench and thread cutter, $50.00 – 65.00.

Left: K80, 10" double-ended alligator bolt wrench, $90.00 – 125.00. Right: K60, 9" single end alligator bolt wrench, $75.00 – 100.00.

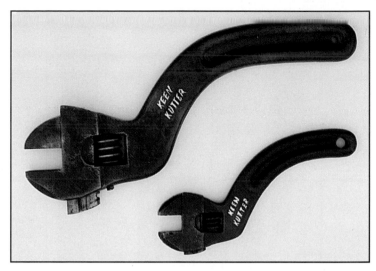

Adjustable "S" wrenches with logo stamped in jaw and "Keen Kutter" written on handle. Left: 6", $275.00 – 350.00. Right: 10", $175.00 – 225.00.

Wrench boxes. Two different labeled wooden boxes, 4¾" wide x 11¼" long x 4" deep. They held six KB10 Black Jack solid handle wrenches, $65.00 – 85.00 each.

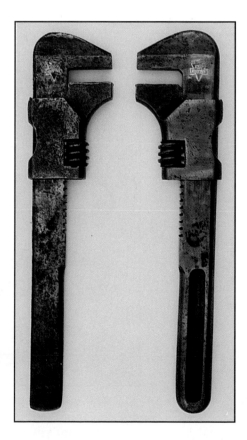

Left:
Bicycle wrench, K94, $65.00 – 85.00.

Right:
Automobile wrenches. Left: K96 with pry on the end, $75.00 – 100.00. Right: K95, $75.00 – 100.00.

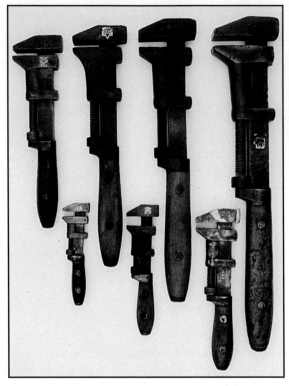

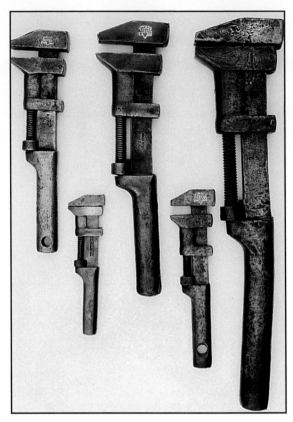

Screw wrenches with wood handles, logo on wrench. 6", $65.00 – 85.00; 8", $50.00 – 70.00; 10", $40.00 – 60.00; 12", $40.00 – 60.00; 15", $40.00 – 60.00; 18", $50.00 – 70.00; 21", $60.00 – 80.00.

Wrenches, all steel with logo. 6", $50.00 – 75.00; 8", $40.00 – 60.00; 10", $40.00 – 60.00; 12", $40.00 – 60.00; 18", $50.00 – 70.00.

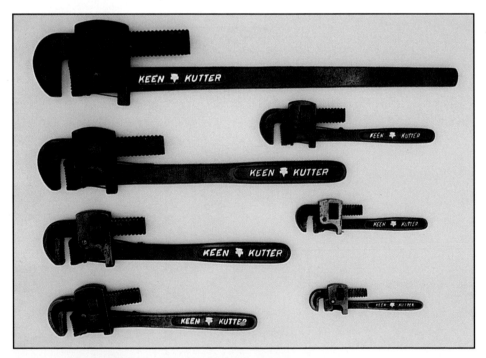

Pipe wrenches with Keen Kutter written on the handle. 6", $75.00 – 125.00; 8", $35.00 – 45.00; 10", $30.00 – 40.00; 12", $25.00 – 35.00; 14", $25.00 – 35.00; 18", $30.00 – 40.00; 24", $50.00 – 75.00.

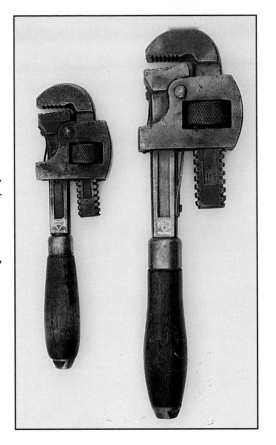

Left:
Pipe wrenches with wooden handles.
Left: 8", $45.00 – 65.00; 10", $40.00 –
50.00.

Right:
Pipe wrench, inserted jaw. KW8, 8",
$45.00 – 55.00.

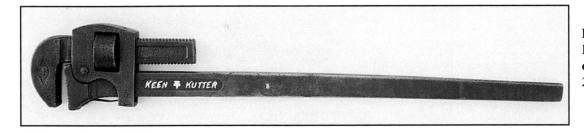

Pipe wrench, 36", with
Keen Kutter written
on handle, $125.00 –
200.00.

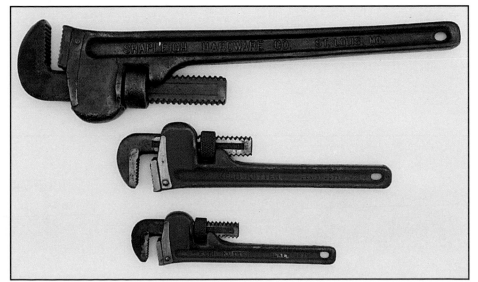

Pipe wrenches, Shapleigh. Top: 18"
$25.00 – 35.00; 10", $30.00 – 40.00; 8",
$30.00 – 40.00.

Angle adjustable wrenches, E. C. Simmons Keen Kutter. Top: 10", $45.00 – 60.00; 8", $45.00 – 60.00; 6", $50.00 – 65.00; 4", $300.00 – 375.00 (rare).

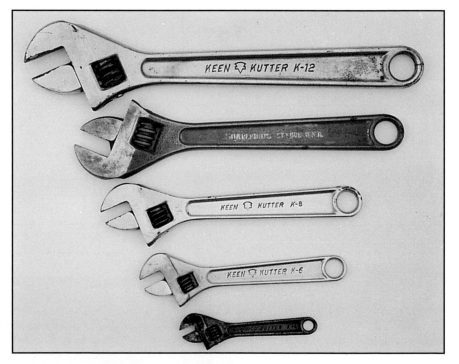

Adjustable wrenches, Shapleigh Keen Kutter. Top: K12, $40.00 – 50.00; K10, $35.00 – 40.00; K8, $30.00 – 35.00; K6, $35.00 – 45.00; K4, $175.00 – 225.00.

Adjustable wrench, 6", another version of a Shapleigh adjustable wrench. There are some other versions also, $30.00 – 35.00.

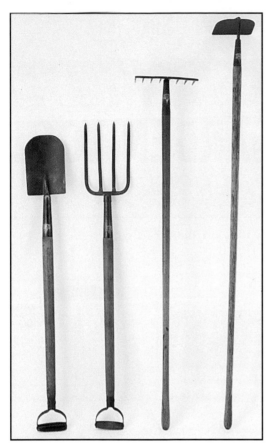

Junior garden set, four pieces, shovel, spading fork, rake, and hoe, $250.00 – 300.00 set.

Garden tool rack, three shelves, "Keen Kutter" embossed on top front shelf. Legs are made from shovel handles, $150.00 – 200.00.

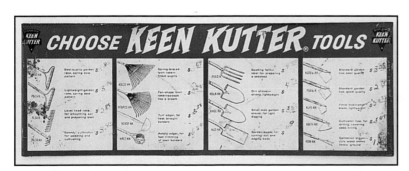

Lawn and garden sign, metal, for rakes, hoes, and shovels, has turned edges to slip on display, 6½" x 18", $75.00 – 100.00.

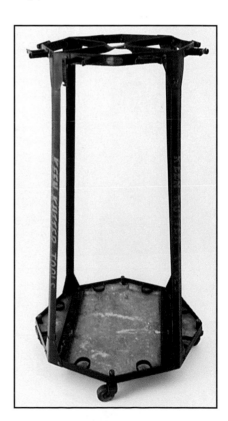

Steel goods display stand, octagon shape, 37¼" tall on rollers, holds eight garden tools on outside and four on inside, $175.00 – 225.00.

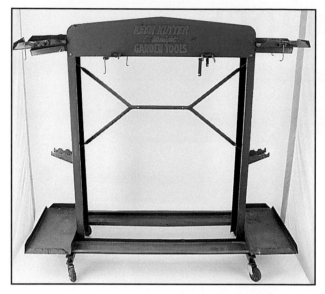

Garden tool rack, metal, $150.00 – 175.00.

Garden tool, cardboard hanging sign, 9" x 14", $75.00 – 125.00.

Garden tool metal rack, 4' long x 6" wide, fastens directly to wall, $100.00 – 125.00.

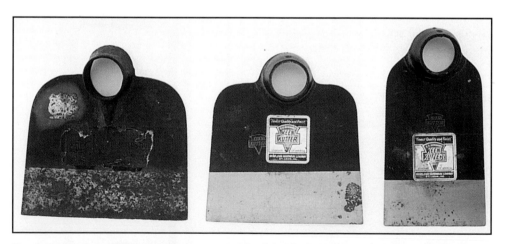

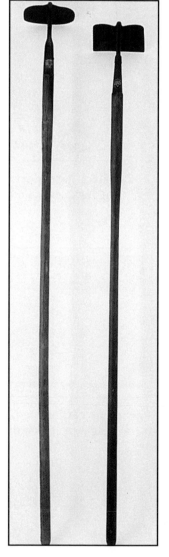

Eye hoes. Left to right: Scovil pattern with old shield emblem, $65.00 – 75.00; Scovil pattern 6¾" wide planter, $65.00 – 75.00; sprouting 4½" wide, $65.00 – 75.00.

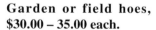

Garden or field hoes, $30.00 – 35.00 each.

Left:
Eye hoes, 4½", $30.00 – 40.00; eye hoes, 4", $30.00 – 40.00; garden mattock hoe, $45.00 – 55.00; weeding hoe, GC 4½", $30.00 – 40.00.

Right:
Reversible lawn rake 24 teeth, 12 loops, $45.00 – 65.00; leaf rake KBR22, $30.00 – 35.00.

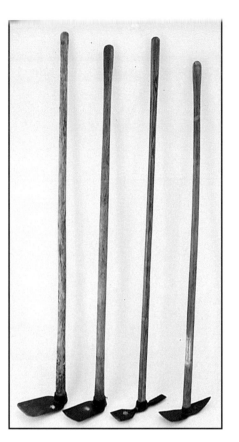

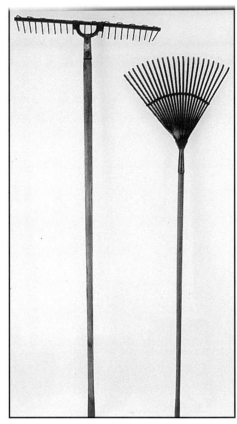

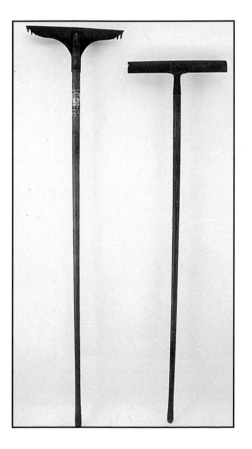

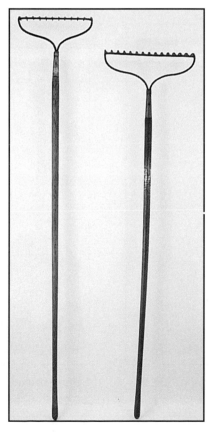

Left:
Dandelion rakes, $30.00 – 45.00 each.

Right:
Garden rakes, $30.00 – 35.00 each.

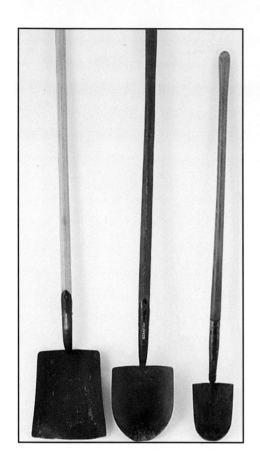

Left:
Dirt shovel, square point, $20.00 – 30.00; dirt shovel, round point, $20.00 – 30.00; garden shovel, K7, $50.00 – 65.00.

Right:
Ditch spades, four different, $25.00 – 30.00 each.

Dirt shovel, wood handle, square point, $35.00 – 45.00. Dirt shovel, metal handle, square point, $20.00 – 25.00. Dirt spade, $20.00 – 25.00.

Scoop shovel, all wood handle, $45.00 – 50.00. Scoop shovel, metal handle, $25.00 – 30.00. Grain scoop, small, $25.00 – 30.00.

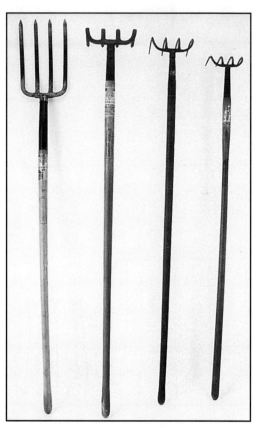

Left:
Rock, sand, and gravel scoop, $50.00 – 75.00. Dirt shovel KRD2B, $25.00 – 35.00.

Right:
Spading fork KHSL, $65.00 – 85.00. Potato hook, $45.00 – 65.00. Potato hook, $30.00 – 35.00. Speedy cultivator, $45.00 – 65.00.

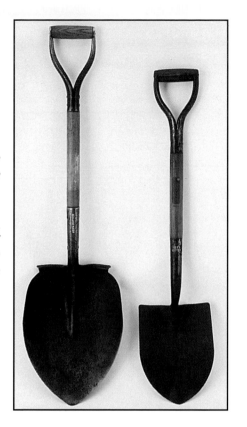

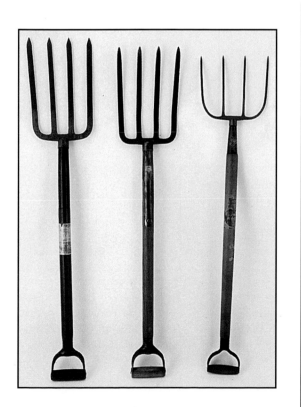

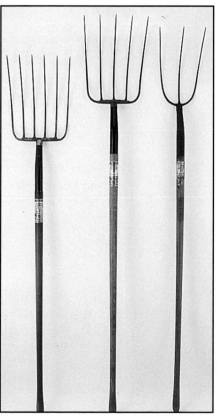

Left:
Spading fork, KHSD, $35.00 – 45.00. Spading fork, $35.00 – 45.00. Baling press fork, $65.00 – 85.00.

Right:
Barley utility fork, K604, 6 tines, $65.00 – 85.00. Barley utility fork, K504½, 5 tines, $65.00 – 85.00. Hay fork, KB304½, 3 tines, $50.00 – 60.00.

Left: Barn or ensilage fork, KCHO, 8 tines, $40.00 – 60.00. Right: Ensilage fork, 8 tines, $35.00 – 40.00.

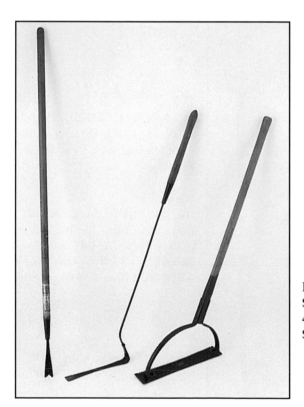

Left to right: Dandelion weeder, $35.00 – 40.00. Grass cutter, $35.00 – 40.00. Weed cutter, KWCS-K, $35.00 – 40.00.

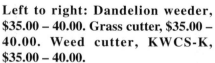

Bush scythe, 18", mint with paper sticker, $100.00 – 150.00; if used, $20.00 – 25.00.

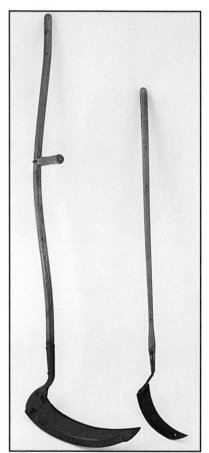

Left: Brush scythe, $35.00 – 45.00. Right: Scythe hook, $30.00 – 35.00.

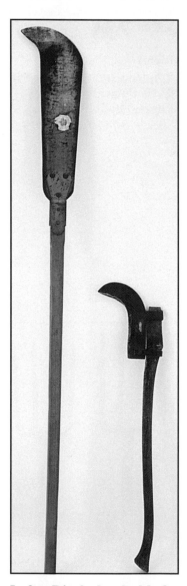

Left: Ditch bank blade, socket pattern, 17" overall length, $50.00 – 75.00. Right: Bush hook, $40.00 – 50.00.

Left:
Left: Post hole digger, $25.00 – 30.00. Right: Post hole auger, $35.00 – 40.00.

Right:
Left to right: Drain cleaner, blade adjusts to any angle, $100.00 – 125.00. Mortar hoe, KPM10, $30.00 – 35.00. Side-walk scraper or scuffle hoe, K7, $35.00 – 45.00.

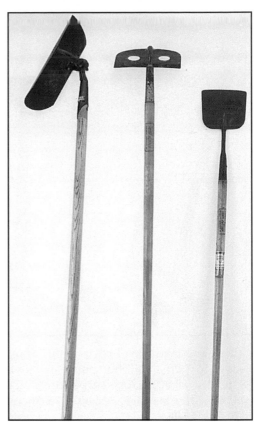

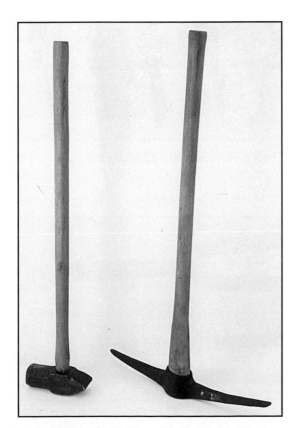

Left: Sledge, $125.00 – 150.00. Right: Garden pick, $25.00 – 30.00.

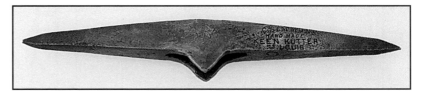

Pick, hand made, 13½" long, $75.00 – 100.00.

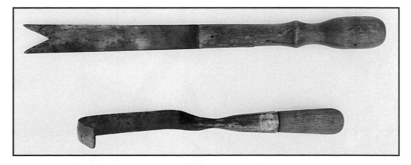

Top: Asparagus knife or lawn weeder, 7¾" blade, $40.00 – 60.00. Bottom: Garden weeder, bent ⅞" wide blade, bent socket, overall length 11", $40.00 – 60.00.

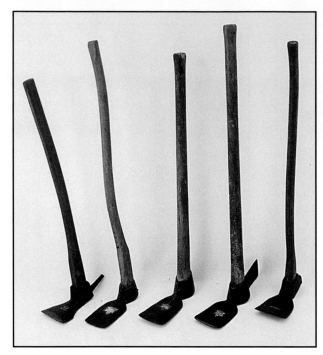

Adzes and mattocks. Left to right: Ship carpenter's adze, $75.00 – 100.00; house carpenter's adze, $30.00 – 40.00; house carpenter's adze, $30.00 – 40.00; cutter mattock, $50.00 – 75.00; railroad adze, $50.00 – 75.00.

Garden weeder, 12½'' long, $15.00 – 30.00. Garden fork, hand held, $15.00 – 30.00. Garden trowel, bent neck, 13'', $50.00 – 75.00. Garden trowel, straight neck, 13'', $50.00 – 75.00.

Grass shears, $10.00 – 20.00 each.

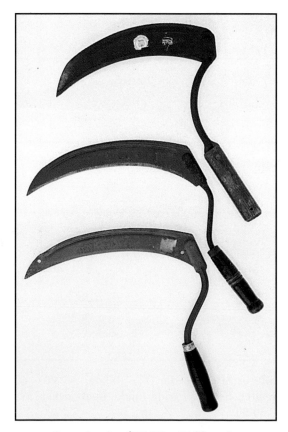

Grass hooks, $15.00 – 35.00 each.

Top: Hedge shears, KS, 8½'', $15.00 – 25.00. Bottom: Long pruning, $30.00 – 35.00.

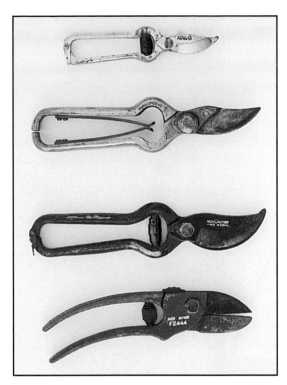

Top to bottom: Ladies pruning shears, K25, 6'' long, $65.00 – 85.00. Pruning shears, K200, 8½'' long, $25.00 – 35.00. Pruning shears with ratchet tightening nut, KCP, 9'' long, $25.00 – 35.00. Pruning shears with bent handles, F2444, 8'', $25.00 – 35.00.

Garden hose label, cardboard, 14'' x 3'', $45.00 – 65.00.

Gas cans, sizes 2½, 5, and 1-gallon, $25.00 – 65.00 each.

Sprayer, 1½-gallon, $75.00 – 100.00.

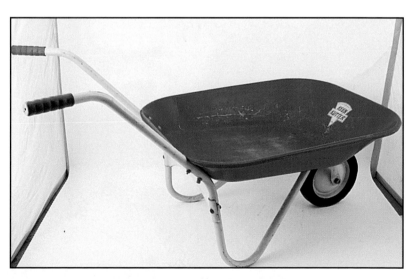

Wheelbarrow, $125.00 – 150.00.

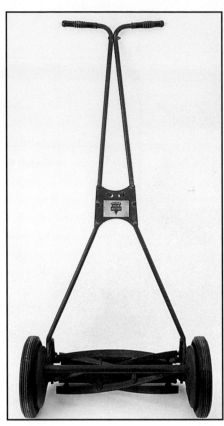

Left:
Lawn cart, $50.00 – 75.00.

Right:
Lawn mower, revolving reel, four blades, KK60, 16" cut, $30.00 – 40.00.

Left:
Lawn mower, revolving reel, five blades, 16" cut, $30.00 – 40.00.

Right:
Lawn trimmer, revolving reel, four knives, 8" cut, $75.00 – 125.00.

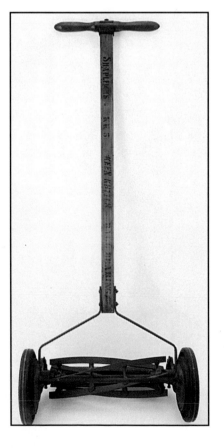

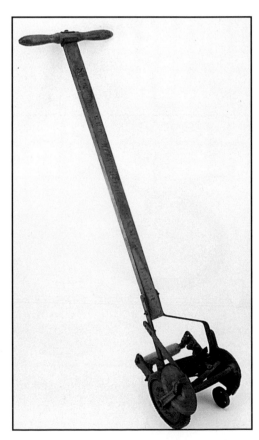

Lawn mower, gas power, KKRA18
855, $75.00 – 100.00.

Rotary tiller, 2¼-HP, $100.00 – 125.00.

Grass catcher for power mower, $25.00 – 35.00.

TAP & DIE SETS

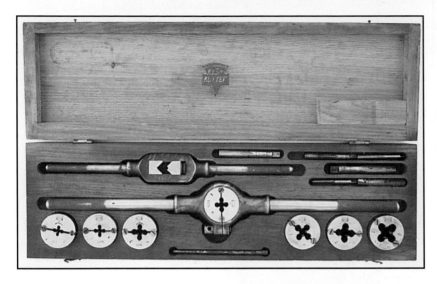

Screw plates (tap and die set) No. K33, complete with seven sizes, taper taps, dies, and guide, stock 22" long, in wooden box, $500.00 – 750.00.

Screw plates (tap and die sets) K31, complete with five sizes, taper taps, dies, and guides, stock 18" long, wooden box, $500.00 – 750.00; K30, complete with five sizes, taper taps, dies, and guides, stock 6" long, wooden box, $300.00 – 500.00.

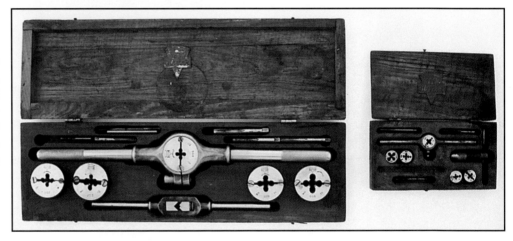

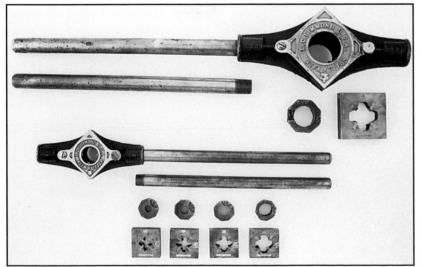

Pipe stock and dies, No. 2, came with five different cutters, ¾", 1", 1¼", 1½", and 2", square size 4", $175.00 – 200.00; pipe stock and dies, No. 1, came with six different cutters, ⅛", ¼", ⅜", ½", ¾", and 1", square size 2½", $175.00 – 200.00.

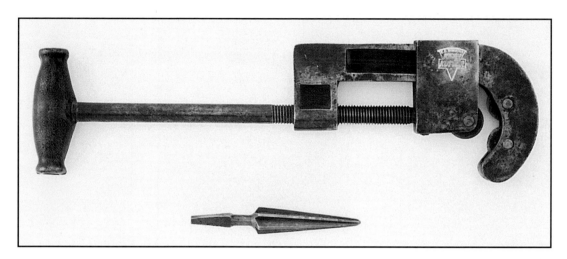

Top: **K2 pipe cutter, three wheel pattern from ¼'' to 2'' capacity, $75.00 – 100.00. Bottom: K126 fluted reamer, cuts from ⅜'' to ⅞'', overall length 5¼'', $35.00 – 45.00.**

Left to right: Pipe vise, KP200, ⅛'' – 2'' capacity, $75.00 – 125.00. Pipe vise, KP412, ⅛'' – 4½'' capacity, $100.00 – 150.00. Pipe vise, KP312, ⅛'' – 3½'' capacity, $75.00 – 100.00

MISCELLANEOUS

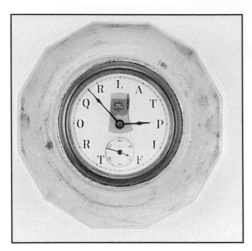

Desk clock, old shield axe head logo. Dial has slogan letters in place of numbers. On the glass, the slogan "The Recollection Of Quality Remains Long After The Price Is Forgotten," is etched. It is 3½" in diameter and has wind-up works, $2,000.00 – 2,500.00.

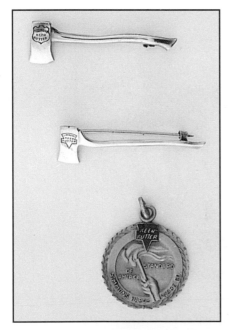

Axe-shaped lapel pin with shield emblem, $200.00 – 225.00; axe-shaped lapel pin, regular emblem, $200.00 – 250.00; watch fob for vest coat, 10KGF, Standard Of America, with salesman's name on back, $250.00 – 300.00.

Pocket watch, achievement award, Elgin, 21 jewels, 14K solid gold, dated Dec. 1938, $2,500.00.

Axe head-shaped jewelry. Left to right: Cuff links, old shield emblem, $350.00 – 450.00; lapel pin, old shield emblem, $150.00 – 200.00; pin for chain, old shield emblem, $125.00 – 175.00; lapel pin, logo shaped, $125.00 – 175.00.

Top row (left to right): 1¼" old shield axe head logo, pinback, $75.00 – 125.00; 1¼" round logo pinback, $75.00 – 100.00; ⅞" round logo, pinback, $50.00 – 75.00; ¾" round logo, pinback, $50.00 – 75.00. Bottom row: Two round ¾" button style, one has black background, $50.00 – 75.00 each. Small pinback that came off knife box, $25.00 – 35.00.

Pinback, celluloid, ⅞", button style with ribbon, $75.00 – 100.00. Pinback, celluloid, ⅞", pin style with ribbon and motto ribbon, $100.00 – 150.00.

Axe head paperweights, 1½" x 3¼", top reads "Compliments of Simmons Hardware." Left: old shield emblem, $300.00 – 325.00 due to good condition with complete nickeling still on it. Right: As is, $150.00 – 175.00; with complete nickeling, $300.00 – 325.00.

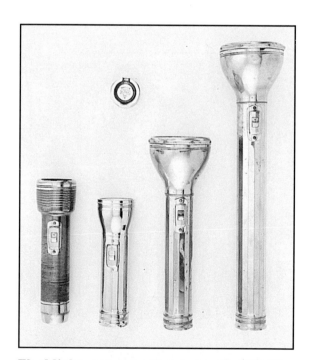

Watch fob, authentic, 1⅛" wide x 1½" tall, slogan on the back. The letters "LE" on the bottom point on the back side verify it as an original. $175.00 – 225.00.

Puzzle with box. Average price, $1,000.00 – 1,300.00; auction price, $1,800.00.

Flashlight, copper color, two-cell, $75.00 – 100.00. Set of three flashlights with same octagonal shape; two, three, and five-cell models, $75.00 – 125.00 each. (Battery end cap with Keen Kutter logo shown.)

Flashlight batteries, Shapleigh, $75.00 – 100.00 each. Left: Green paper cover. Right: Red metal.

Sealed beam lantern, Shapleigh Hardware Co., uses a 6-volt battery, $45.00 – 65.00.

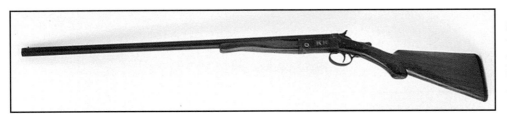

Shotgun, 16 gauge, marked "Simmons Hardware" in two places and has KK on side of gun, $200.00 – 500.00. There were also other gauges.

Holster, leather, for gun. Logo in lower left corner, $125.00 – 150.00.

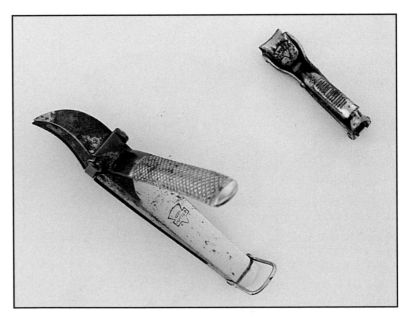

Left: Toe nail clippers, $70.00 – 80.00. Right: Nail clippers, patent 8-16-1910, $55.00 – 75.00.

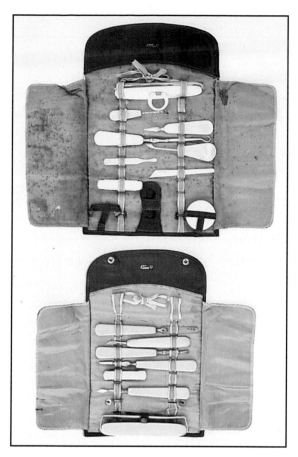

Manicure sets with roll up leather cases, marking only on the cases, $100.00 – 150.00 each.

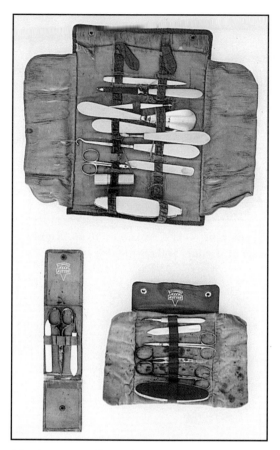

Manicure sets. Large leather roll-up with silk inside. Scissors, shoe horn, and nail file are marked, $100.00 – 150.00. Small three-piece fold-up, two items marked, $75.00 – 100.00. Leather six-piece roll-up with three scissors marked, $75.00 – 100.00.

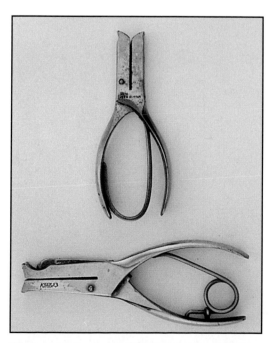

Ticket punches, two different styles, $75.00 – 100.00 each.

Painter's cap, E. C. Simmons, size 7⅛". This was a store give-away. $75.00 – 100.00.

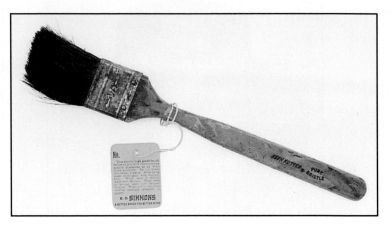

Left: Varnish, one pint, S-417, $80.00 – 110.00. Right: Paint, one quart of shellac, $60.00 – 80.00.

Paint brush, 1½", $100.00 – 150.00. Tag for paint brush, $15.00.

Cloth sack, drawstring, used to cover handles of long-handled tools during shipment. Measures 17" wide x 44" long, $175.00 – 225.00.

Cloth sack used to cover tools during shipment, 9" wide x 30" long, $50.00 – 75.00.

Boy's wagon, Jet, $200.00 – 250.00.

Boy's wagon, Rocket, $200.00 – 250.00.

Keen Kaster No. SKK Reel, Simmons Hardware Co., $35.00 – 55.00.

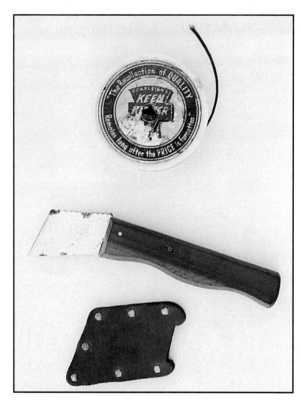

Top: Spool of fishing string, $40.00 – 45.00; mint condition, $100.00 – 150.00. Bottom: Fish knife with leather sheath. It is an S-K72A short blade 1¾'' long x 1¼'' wide. One saw edge for scaling, other edge and front for cutting, $40.00 – 60.00.

Minnow bucket, Shapleigh, 9'' x 9½'' diameter, $150.00 – 175.00.

Left:
Eraser, should have a handle, $125.00 – 175.00. (Used for ink or pencil removal before the type we have today.)

Right:
Small child's toy electric stove, Shapleigh, 8" tall x 8¼" wide x 4½" depth, $350.00 – 450.00.

Cigar box for 100 cigars, 5½" x 9" x 5", $175.00 – 250.00; cigar boxes for 50 cigars, 5½" x 8¾" x 2½", $175.00 – 250.00 each. The one in the back center has the display glass lid which has wording: "Keen Kutter 5 cents Cigar 5 cents," value of glass, $200.00 – 250.00.

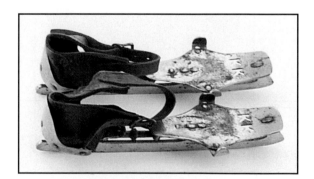

Ice skates, Klipper Klub, $30.00 – 40.00.

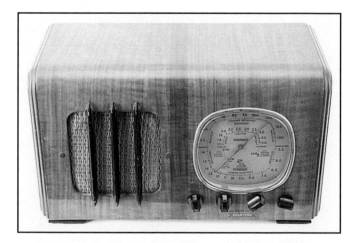

Radio, electric "Keen Tone," E. C. Simmons, $200.00 – 400.00. There are several different models and styles of the radio.

REPRODUCTIONS & FAKES

Thermometer, reproduction. Biggest difference is the variance of temperature. The original only goes from -30° to 120°. The reproduction goes from -60° to 140°. The reproduction also has a smaller spring on the back.

Reproduction sign: Keen Kutter Tools. 7½" x 21", designed like the original hardware store advertising signs that were 9¾" x 27¾".

Reproduction sign: 12" x 12" tin sign that was taken from the left side of the original 9¾" x 27¾" store sign with hardware store name on it.

Reproduction sign: "We Sell." This tin 10½" x 15½" black/red/white sign is a remake from the large porcelain flanged double sided. The bottom right corner has the name AAA Sign Co., Coitsville, OH.

Reproduction sign: "We Sell Genuine Keen Kutter," 8½" x 11" porcelain. It is white with red and black lettering. This is also made in tin with painted letters.

Reproduction poster: "The Dog Doesn't Mind He Knows It Won't Hurt – It's A Keen Kutter," 27" x 22". Also came in size 17½" x 21½". These were made from either the magazine advertisement or the actual postcard version.

Fake boot jack, shaped like a crab. Cast iron, has "Keen Kutter" written underneath.

Fake cast iron match holder, 6¾" x 4¼", the holder part sticks out 1½". Usually red but some were green background with red logo and some had yellow letters.

Small waffle iron, reproduction. These started surfacing in the first part of 1988. They are identical to the original one that has the E. C. Simmons logo inside with the exception of the 3⅞" griddle size and the wooden handle. The original handle has a wire twist. Some people call these salesman's samples. Some are selling at outrageous prices as original. BEWARE!

Watch fobs, all four are reproductions. The original should have the maker's emblem on back.

Reproduction padlock, front and back view with key. Lock looks very crude. The key is a barrel type with a hole in the middle.

Reproduction emblems. Top: Cast iron. Bottom: Brass.

Left to right: Reproduction watch fob, green one with strap, back reads "coin silver," has slogan, Shapleigh Hardware Co., St. Louis, MO; watch fob, back reads "sterling," has the slogan, Shapleigh Hardware Co., St. Louis, MO.

Plumb bob, reproduction. Solid brass, no solid brass was ever known to be made originally. The logo on the reproduction is usually short and wide. These are coming out of the St. Louis area.

Reproductions of butcher's apron and slaw cutter. It appears someone made a stamp of the logo and did both of these.

What is a Keen Kutter reproduction?

A new version or copy of an original item that was manufactured and distributed by Simmons Hardware and Shapleigh Hardware.

Other reproduction items not pictured:

Nail apron: Date is stamped on apron, 1982 era.

Pocket knives: Cold stamped.

Glass paperweights: Contain pictures of the puzzle, clock, or even letterhead.

Brass tags for wooden ice box: White clad Simmons Hardware Co.

Brass tags: For Leader - Simmons Hardware Co.

Showcases: Especially small ones, etching of logo on the glass is very hard to distinguish in some cases.

Postcard: Advertising the 1915 San Francisco E. C. Simmon's Keen Kutter Exhibit at the Panama-Pacific International Exposition Manufacturers Palace, 7" x 10½".

What is a "fake" or "fantasy item" in Keen Kutter?

An item bearing the Keen Kutter name or trademark never originally manufactured or distributed by Simmons Hardware or Shapleigh Hardware .

Additional "fake"or "fantasy" items not pictured:

Axe: Small, approximately 2" overall length, metal head with a wooden carved handle. These are coming out of the St. Louis area.

Pocket watch: Plain nickel case, has a poor quality image. (As far as I know, pocket watches were given to employees for service awards, but not manufactured for resale. They were usually made of gold and produced by watch companies such as Elgin.)

Family scales: Has two Keen Kutter red logos on each side of the pointer on the front as well as red logos on the side. If the logo is paper, I'd say it is definitely a fake. I've never seen a scale with Keen Kutter on it, even in the catalogs. There are several different versions of the Simmons scales.

Alarm clock: Has paper dial with two Keen Kutter logos.

Marble: White with red logo. (I have seen only on the Internet.)

Mirror: Small 2" round pocket mirror with Keen Kutter in the logo and the slogan around it.

VAL-TEST ITEMS

Left:
Val-Test tin sign, 29½" x 29½", $100.00 – 150.00.

Right:
Val-Test tin sign, 29½" x 29½", $100.00 – 150.00.

Val-Test electric clock with plastic face, 15" x 50", $250.00 – 350.00.

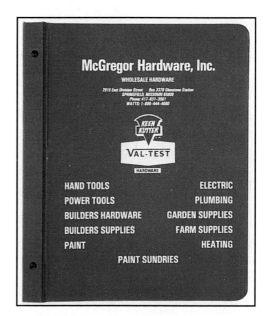

Val-Test Hardware catalog, eight sections with index and price list, $75.00 – 100.00.

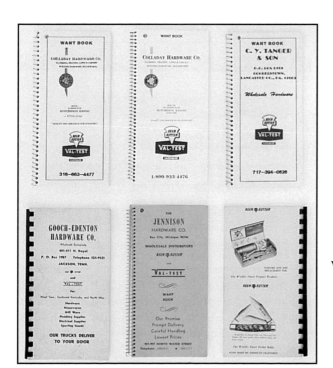

Val-Test want books, $15.00 – 20.00 each.

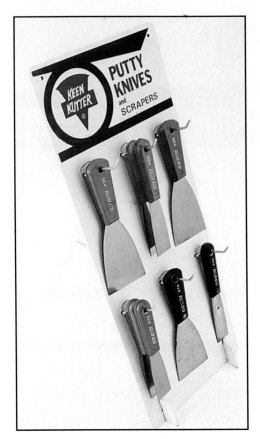

Val-Test nail set displays. Both are 6½" x 5½" with 24 holes. One has name written on it, and other has name on paper label applied. Display without nail sets, $45.00 – 65.00 each.

Val-Test chisel and punch display. 9¾" x 4½" with 30 holes. One has the name written on it, and one has name on applied paper label. Display without punches, $45.00 – 65.00 each.

Val-Test putty knives and scrapers easel back display, without knives, $100.00. Putty knives and scrapers, $15.00 – 25.00 each.

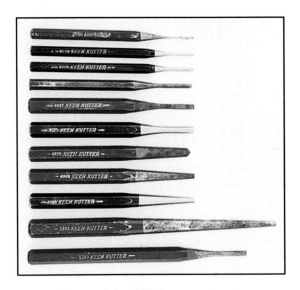

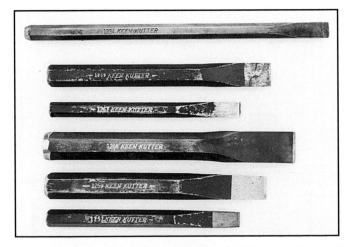

Machine punches, various sizes, $10.00 – 20.00 each. These were some of the last ones made by Shapleigh. Val-Test distributed remaining stock plus had some made with "Keen Kutter" written out following the same numbering system.

Cold chisels, various sizes, $10.00 – 20.00 each. Some of the last ones Shapleigh made. Val-Test distributed remaining stock, also made others with "Keen Kutter" written out following the same numbering system.

Val-Test spray paint cans, $7.00 – 10.00 each. Val-Test cardboard sign advertising paint, $40.00 – 60.00.

Val-Test propane torch kits. Kits, $25.00 – 45.00 each; tank alone, $5.00 – 8.00.

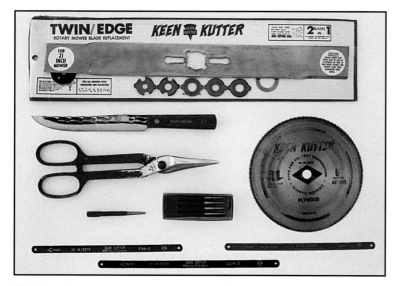

Val-Test items: lawn mower blade, $20.00 – 25.00; 8" butcher knife, $10.00 – 15.00; tin snips, $20.00 – 25.00; full box of twelve nail sets, $75.00 – 100.00; 8" saw blade, $10.00 – 15.00; hacksaw blades, $4.00 – 8.00 each.

Right:
Spark plug, manufactured for Val-Test Dist., Chicago, IL. Fits a K17M power mower, $75.00 – 100.00.

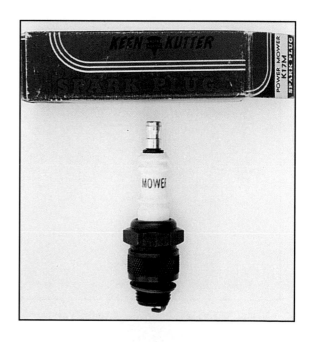

Val-Test yard stick, $15.00 – 20.00.

Val-Test gas can, 2½-gallon, $15.00 – 20.00.

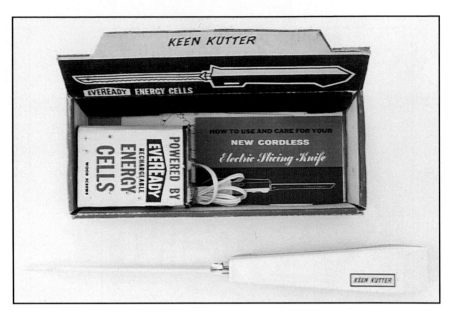

Val-Test electric knife, cordless, rechargeable, $50.00 – 60.00.

Val-Test nail apron, $30.00 – 60.00.

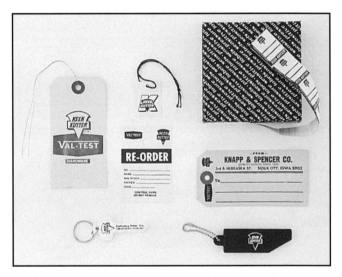

Val-Test items: shipping tags, $3.00 – 4.00 each; tie-on price tag, $1.00; box of stick-on labels, $10.00 – 15.00; re-order form, $1.00 – 2.00; give-away key chains, $10.00 – 15.00 each.

Val-Test saber saw, K-431T1, $15.00.

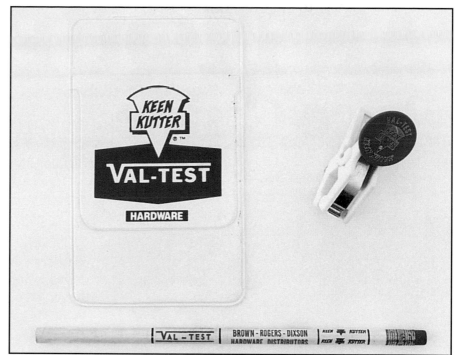

Val-Test give-away advertisement items: pocket saver, $15.00 – 20.00; clip, $15.00 – 20.00; pencil, $10.00 – 15.00.

CLUB INFORMATION

MID-WEST TOOL COLLECTORS ASSOCIATION, INC. (M-WTCA)

M-WTCA is a non-profit national organization founded in May 1968. Its purpose is to promote the preservation, study, and understanding of ancient tools, implements, and devices of the farm, home industry, and shop of the pioneers; to study the crafts in which these objects were used and the craftsmen who used them; to share knowledge and understanding with others, especially where it may benefit restorations, museums and like institutions. Annual membership is $35.00.

THE HARDWARE COMPANIES KOLLECTORS KLUB (THCKK)

THCKK is a non-profit organization formed in March 1996. Its purpose is to distribute and provide information about early hardware companies such as E. C. Simmons and Shapleigh Hardware and various brands of tools such as Keen Kutter, Diamond Edge, Winchester, Blue Grass, OVB, etc. Another purpose is to keep the members informed of any known fakes or reproductions. Presently THCKK has approximately 225 members representing several states. Dues are $15.00 per year and includes 4 newsletters. A yearly convention involving tail-gating and member consignment auction is held usually the last weekend in March, normally in Henrietta, MO, which is open to the general public.

For more information concerning M-WTCA or THCKK, mail requests to Jerry & Elaine Heuring, 28450 US Highway 61, Scott City, MO 63780 or e-mail jheuring@igateway.net.

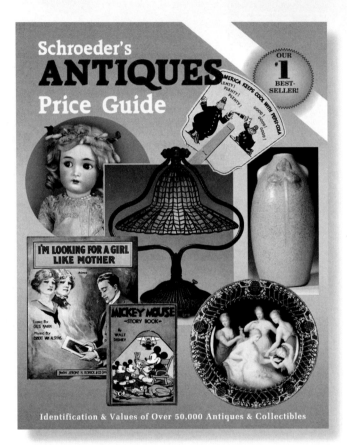